God Calls
a People

God Calls a People:

A Journey Through the Old Testament

By Sister Blanche Twigg, M.H.S.H.

Nihil Obstat
> Rev. Hilarion Kistner, O.F.M.
> Rev. Eugene H. Maly

Imprimi Potest
> Rev. Andrew Fox, O.F.M.
> Provincial

Imprimatur
> +Joseph L. Bernardin
> Archbishop of Cincinnati
> June 1, 1978

Cover Illustration *Moses Receiving the Tablets of the Law* (Exodus 20:21-22), color lithograph, 1956, by Marc Chagall. The Cincinnati Art Museum, Mr. and Mr. Ross W. Sloniker Collection of 20th Century Biblical and Religious Prints.

Cover concept and design by Janet Gruenwald and Michael Reynolds

SBN 0-912228-42-3

Contents

Introduction   1

Chapter 1
The World of the Bible and Its Gods   5

Chapter 2
The Bible: A Faith Perspective   25

Chapter 3
The Bible: Story of Salvation   37

Chapter 4
Filling In Old Testament Salvation Events   61

Chapter 5
Genesis 1—11 and Its Questions   79

Chapter 6
The Prophet: The Man Appointed by Yahweh   97

Chapter 7
Law: The Will of Yahweh   119

Chapter 8
Wisdom: An Approach to the Good Life   143

Conclusion   163

But this is the covenant which I will make with the house of Israel after those days, says the LORD. I will place my law within them, and write it upon their hearts; I will be their God, and they shall be my people.

Jeremiah 31:33

Introduction

God Calls a People: A Journey Through the Old Testament is addressed to a wide audience:

- young adults or high school students who wish to get to know *the book;*
- adults who wish to acquire a background out of which to intelligently approach the Bible;
- Christians who would like to put the readings of the liturgy in perspective;
- persons eager to get back to the roots of their Christian traditions;
- study groups whose interests or aims fit into any one of the above categories.

This volume does not pretend to offer a scholarly approach to the Bible. Its intent, rather, is a pastoral one. Such an approach aims to deepen the reader's faith in a God who speaks to a human audience as well as the reader's respect for the men who, in times long past, listened to this God and struggled to share in human language the word they heard. It also aims to foster an attitude of deepest reverence for this book on the pages of which every man and every woman can come to grips with the problem of salvation.

God Calls a People does not cover the entire Old Testament. Its scope is limited. Nonetheless, it is hoped that the insights offered will provide the reader with a basic tool or mindset readily transferable to the Bible as a whole, and that this will serve as a solid ground for more comprehensive study or reading.

The reader of this book should have at hand at all times a copy of the Bible, preferably the *New American Bible*. (All Bible quotes in this book are taken from this translation.) Chapters and/or verses noted in the text should be read as they are given. Reading *about* the Bible is far less enriching than actually reading the Bible itself. So, do refer constantly to your Bible and to its footnotes.

From scanning chapter titles the reader may be tempted to read chapters in another order than given. For example, Chapter 1, "The World of the Old Testament and Its Gods," may strike some as overly technical. Place it later if you wish. There is, however, a kind of gradation in the development of the material, and missing any part could limit overall comprehension.

Study Guides are set up at the end of each chapter to:

  • enrich the content of the chapter just read;

- direct the reader to focus in on specific Bible verses and/or sections so that the chapter content may be more fully drawn out and exemplified;
- encourage facility in the use of the Bible;
- invite the reader to go beyond the Bible into the *now* situation.

The reader may wish to follow through each of the suggested guides or pick and choose according to need and/or appeal.

The intent behind the writing of *God Calls a People* is more than the desire to make comprehensible the first part of the Bible. The broader hope is that its considerations will stimulate a better knowledge and understanding of the person of Jesus in the New Testament.

The LORD, the God of Israel, says: "I will tear away the kingdom from Solomon's grasp . . . because he has forsaken me and worshiped Astarte, goddess of the Sidonians. . . ."

1 Kings 11:31,33

Chapter 1

The World of the Bible and Its God

An introductory study of the Bible, like the study of any literary or artistic masterpiece, must include a survey of the complex setting out of which it emerged. For while the Bible has traditionally been attributed to a divine author, it is, nonetheless, an "earthy" book. The scenes of biblical activity are geographically located. The people who created the cultures reflected in its pages were real people. The time span it covers was the measured time of human calculation—an open span encompassing the flux and striving of prior generations and, at the same moment, granting the possibility of new and better things.

Therefore, we may not be simplistic about the Bible. Its people emerged into a world already old—

a world marked by the peaceful as well as warlike movements of man and impressed with his cities, farmlands and places of worship, his commerce, art and craftsmanship; a world regulated by laws and a developing sense of justice.

This chapter surveys this complex background. In conclusion, the conflict between the Hebrew God of history and the Canaanite fertility gods is discussed.

Mesopotamia: Home of the Aramean

Then you shall declare before the LORD, your God, "My father was a wandering Aramean who went down to Egypt with a small household and lived there as an alien. But there he became a nation great, strong and numerous. When the Egyptians maltreated and oppressed us, imposing hard labor upon us, we cried to the LORD, the God of our fathers, and he heard our cry and saw our affliction, our toil and our oppression. He brought us out of Egypt with his strong hand and outstretched arm, with terrifying power, with signs and wonders; and bringing us into this country, he gave us this land flowing with milk and honey." (Dt 26:5-9)

In five tightly packed verses, Deuteronomy sweeps through the pre- and early history of Israel, the people the Lord God had claimed as his own. These verses, considered by many scholars as a *creed* recited during a cultic festival, provide a structure for a simple analysis of the setting in and out of which Bible things are rooted.

A basic knowledge of this setting is important. When we confront the multiple geographic, cultural and religious currents which converged in the mind and heart of Israel, we appreciate to a greater extent the richness as well as the complexity of the Bible, the book in which that people tells of its personal saga with God.

Geography and People. The geographical area defined by this creedal statement is known as the Fertile Crescent—that span of fertile land skirting the Arabian desert, reaching from the Persian Gulf up through the plain of the Tigris and Euphrates, curving around through Syria and Palestine, and continuing toward the Nile in Egypt. (See map on p. 8).

Jacob, renamed Israel, is the "wandering Aramean" of the passage. He, as well as the two other patriarchs, Abraham and Isaac, had wandered from Mesopotamia, "the land between the rivers" (the Tigris and the Euphrates, that is). Mesopotamia was a region with mountainous plateaus in the north and marshy regions in the southern valley. Jacob had wandered, first of all, into the land of Canaan and later into Egypt.

We refer to these early Bible people as Hebrews. Not an ethnic designation, the name *Hebrew* denotes a social class. It could well fit the seminomadic Abraham, Isaac and Jacob. The ancestors of the Hebrews were, doubtless, a mixture of many races. The Bible itself records Israel's relationship to Moab, Ammon and Edom and to a number of Arabian tribes. There was, however, a strong feeling of kinship with the Arameans because both Israel and the later Arameans were of a common ethnic and linguistic stock. Among those who adopted the Ara-

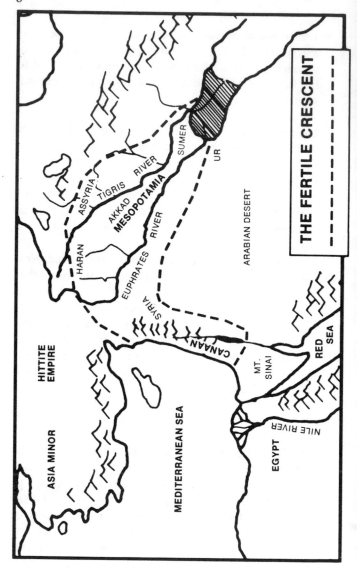

THE FERTILE CRESCENT

mean language and who were Israel's more immediate kin were the "Westerners" (Amorites) who dwelt along the upper Euphrates and its tributaries.

Even earlier than the "Westerners," a people known as the Akkadians had claimed upper Mesopotamia as home. Through intermarriage with the later Amorites, their blood, too, flowed in the veins of the people who became Israel.

The Sumerians in the lower valley may have been of northern and Asiatic origin. The civilization they created had an impact throughout a great part of the ancient world—especially among their neighbors in upper Mesopotamia.

As early as 4000 B.C., the Sumerians had begun to build a system of dikes and canals designed to control the periodic flooding of the Tigris and Euphrates Rivers. Intelligent irrigation turned hitherto dry plains into orchards, vegetable gardens and grain fields. This agricultural base gave rise to a strong political state.

Buildings of monumental proportion were constructed. Processes for pounding, then pouring copper were developed. The use of solid-wheeled vehicles and ovens for firing pottery evidenced a remarkable technical mastery. Before the closing centuries of the fourth millennium, some 2,000 years before Israel emerged as a people, a style of writing—now called cuneiform—was invented, and a Sumerian literature developed.

Sumerian culture waned in the 24th century B.C. when power passed to the Semitic kings of Akkad. Several centuries later it enjoyed a renaissance, but finally played itself out after having run a magnificent course for over 1,500 years.

Religion and the State. The ancient Mesopotamians were deeply religious. And because religion was an official state concern, it was constantly in the foreground of life: in daily behavior, in every activity and in all situations.

Its principal characteristic was the worship of the forces of nature and the sources of life. The gods were concerned, therefore, with the motive powers of the world and the fertility of plants, animals and men. The sun and the moon, the rain and the storm, the river and its floods were all connected in one way or the other with the gods. So also were the animals symbolic of the mystery of sex, especially the serpent and the bull. The gods were thought of as either male or female and as having very human, often base, manners.

Places of worship were built everywhere. Babylon alone contained 53 temples, of which the greatest was the temple of Marduk. A common form of religious structure was the *ziggarut,* a pointed tower built in tiers. (The biblical Tower of Babel was, no doubt, such a building.) Here the divinity supposedly visited the people during splendid liturgies. Public rituals were compulsory. In addition, private piety generated many devotions and domestic cults.

The religion was polytheistic and its complexity defies a straightforward analysis. The essential faith, at least of the religious elite, can be summed up thus: A mysterious Reality, divinity, dominates man. Into this "divinity" there merges the plurality of gods. But divinity is expressed in a supreme Will which is superior to all the gods.

The order of the gods was conceived as a

heavenly state on the pattern of a city assembly. But the gods were capricious by nature. Peace and order on earth depended on a balance between divine wills, one which could easily be upset. The function of religious cult (that is, the worship of the gods) was to serve the gods and to appease their wrath.

Mesopotamian religion never rose to the knowledge of a god who transcends the powers of nature or even of man. It was marked by the superstitions of demonology and divination. The Sumerian belief in the afterlife is vague and "The Epic of Gilgamesh" (Sumerian in origin) sounds the note of despair. In the last analysis, the religion was of this world and its good. It promised no more and asked no more than the performance of the cult.

The governmental system was monarchical and the king's power was understood as coming from the gods. An ordered bureaucracy permitted the central authority to exercise power throughout the various kingdoms which later developed into empires.

Literature. Mesopotamian literature covers the gamut of bookkeeping notes, contracts, agricultural hymns, business and private correspondence, registry records, magic formulas, laws, prayers, poems, a kind of proverbs, and wisdom writing. The most characteristic and important writings are epics with a heroic and mythological theme. Two celebrated works with importance for Old Testament study are "Enuma Elish" (a poem) and "The Epic of Gilgamesh."

Egypt: Land of Sojourn and Hard Labor

Genesis 47 gives the details of the settlement of Jacob and his sons in the land of Goshen in Egypt. The Deuteronomy passage above says only that Jacob "went down to Egypt." The move was prompted by a severe famine in Canaan and would have occurred roughly around 1750 B.C. When the author of Exodus writes of the situation of the "descendants of Jacob" (about 1250 B.C.), he speaks of these descendants in two ways: as Israelites and as Hebrews.

Geography and People. In ancient times the political geography of Egypt included the valley of the Nile, the dry wastes of the Libyan desert on the west, and the Arabian desert on the east—between the Nile and the Red Sea.

The origins of the ancient Egyptians are hidden in prehistory. Possibly the earliest native population was Hamitic African. Sometime in prehistory Semites from western Asia invaded the land and merged with the natives into a single type.

While the development of civilization in Mesopotamia had many ups and downs, that of Egypt apparently followed a smooth course. Mesopotamia was the scene of many population shifts occasioned by invasions from the north. Egypt, on the other hand, was relatively isolated from the rest of the Near East. This plus the stability created by the Nile River with its regular and fertilizing floods made for harmonious living conditions. Before Egypt emerged into history in the 29th century B.C., social and political unity was already achieved and a system of writing called hieroglyphics was in use.

Around 2600 B.C., the classical period of Egyptian civilization began. This was the age of the pyramids. Government was strong; administration well-organized. Commerce was active along the river, on land and at sea. Religious architecture flourished and the clergy held a high place in society. The picture of Egypt at this early age of history was already one of political, artistic and economic grandeur.

Religion and the State. The art and architecture of ancient Egypt witnesses to the importance of religion. Religion was polytheistic and, like that of the Sumerians, its complexity defies analysis. It is even difficult to determine whether the various deities were nature gods or gods of nation, tribe or clan.

The great deities were solar gods, the most important of which was Ra. Almost as important as Ra was Osiris, the god of the dead. The Egyptians had an elaborate belief in the afterlife. It was believed that survival was maintained by mummification. One king, Amenhotep, proposed the worship of a single god, but the worship was resisted and it scarcely outlasted his reign.

The Egyptians' world was a changeless order established at creation and as regular as the Nile floods. The cornerstone of this order was the god-king (the pharaoh) who cared for his people in life and lived on in the world of the gods at death. In theory, all Egypt was his property, all resources were at his disposal; his power was absolute. As god-king the pharaoh upheld justice, but so far no ancient Egyptian law code has been discovered. Probably one was considered unnecessary.

Literature. The remains of Egyptian literature are extensive. Among the types of literary forms are the romance or tale, popular songs and love lyrics, religious hymns, historical narratives depicted by temple inscriptions and wisdom books and collections of maxims and instructions. The influence of this early Egyptian wisdom literature upon the "wisdom" of the Bible is significant.

Canaan: Land of Promise

And finally, " . . . [the Lord] gave us this land flowing with milk and honey" (Dt 26:9). The "land" is Canaan; and "milk and honey" possibly refer to two occupations of the land: grazing and vine culture, whence milk and grape honey. The Israelite conquest of this area between Syria and Egypt began under Joshua around 1250 B.C.

Geography and People. Physically, this is a land of variations, irregular and broken up into many divisions. The most striking feature is the central backbone of hill country lying between the Jordan and the Mediterranean coastland. The hill country is cut by the valley of Esdraelon which gives access to the Jordan Valley. Temperatures are uneven. The water supply is meager and, until quite recently, life was governed strictly by the rhythm of the rains. The land has an austere yet ever-changing beauty.

A corridor between Egypt and outer Asia, Canaan belonged first to one, then to another. At the beginning of the 20th century B.C., a population of mixed strains dwelt in the land. Semites from Upper Mesopotamia and the desert regions had migrated there and mixed with the original inhabitants. Pillaging by outsiders and frequent internal rivalry in war had forced these inhabitants to cluster themselves into small fortified groups. For the most part life was crude and poor.

In the period of the Israelite conquest the land was divided into autonomous city-states. These were political centers that embraced a fortified city and a number of satellite cities or villages. Building evidenced a superior workmanship which the Israelites could never duplicate.

Some degree of cultural and technical development was attained in Canaan. But because of so many diverse foreign influences, Canaanite civilization never showed an originality such as that of the Phoenicians, the coastal neighbors to the north.

Language gradually took shape and contributions were made toward the development of an alphabet. Hebrew, the language of the Israelites from their entry into Canaan up to within a few hundred years of the birth of Christ, was a dialect of this Canaanite tongue. Hebrew gradually became a dead language and Aramaic, the language of the Jews' immediate neighbors as well as the official language of the western part of the Persian Empire, ultimately superseded it.

Religion and Worship. With the exception of the Egyptians, the other peoples in the Fertile Crescent are broadly referred to as Semites, supposedly descended from Shem (Gn 10). Semites contributed to the ideas and religious customs of Canaan. The divinity of the Near East was called *El,* but Canaanites preferred the title *Baal.* Baal's consort was variously called Anath or Astarte. Abraham, of course, who originally came from beyond Canaan, used the title *El* in designation of his God.

Nature was personified and adored. Hence divinities were connected with springs and wells, trees and orchards, sex and the rhythm of the seasons. Favorite places of worship were summits or ground elevations, that is, the "high places." These were holy areas occupied by an altar in the center and adorned with stones elevated on carved palings. Certain great high places became sanctuaries—centers for pilgrimage and devotion. Later on we find the Israelites, through their prophets, repudiating the high places as places of unlawful or immoral cult, either of Yahweh or of the gods of the Canaanites.

Music, dancing, frenzy, noise, sensuality, a contagious ecstasy—all held place in Canaanite worship. Sacrifice was the principle act of worship; farm produce, animals and humans (especially children) were offered. In addition, prayers, magical incantations and ritual plays aimed to insure fertility.

At the bottom of such worship was the belief that the annual cycle of fertility was an annual renewal of creation. In this cycle, life was produced from death and the god who produced new life (fertility) must die. But the creative deity rose from death and triumphed over his enemies: the chaos and disorder of the world of nature. Through a new union with his female consort the source of fertility was renewed.

Sacred prostitution was part of this ritual drama. The union of the god and goddess was represented by the high priest (or the king) and priestess. Worshipers also took part in the ritual by union with sacred prostitutes. They believed that through this they achieved communion with the gods and cooperated with the deity in bringing forth new life and order in the world.

Certain burial customs reveal a common belief in survival after death. Tombs, often adjacent to sanctuaries, were venerated, and families and clans met there from time to time. For the Canaanite, the vital energy which animated the living could never be lost.

Thought and Language of the Ancient Near East

He brought us out of Egypt with his strong hand and outstretched arm. (Dt 26:8)

While we Westerners would be inclined to speak in abstractions like "God is omnipotent," the Hebrews, in common with other Semites, preferred to translate reality into concrete words such as those quoted above. They entered into the world they saw, touching and feeling rather than standing apart from it to comment abstractly. They *knew* it, participated in it. And when they expressed themselves, it was in living, graphic, sensual imagery. This is why the story form is the preferred means for speaking about religious beliefs.

Semitic literature grew spontaneously out of the lives of the people—their history and geography, their pastoral way of life, their cruel wars, their laws and institutions. Its most important structural feature as exemplified in the psalms, prophets and wisdom literature is *parallelism*.

In *synonymous* parallelism the poetic line has two members, the second repeating the thought of the first:

> And now, O Kings, give heed;
>> take warning you rulers of the earth.
> Serve the LORD with fear and rejoice before
>> him;
>> with trembling pay homage to him.
>>> (Ps 2:10,11)

In *synthetic* parallelism the balance is one of form:

> I myself have set up my king
>> on Zion, my holy mountain. (Ps 2:6)

And in *antithetic* parallelism, the thought of the first line is reversed:

> For the LORD watches over the way of the
>> just,
>> but the way of the wicked vanishes. (Ps 1:6)

Semitic literature also employed symbolism. This was natural for the Semite to whom the whole of reality, of thought and of life is a symbol. The highest development of the Semitic use of symbol was the parable. (See 2 Sm 12:1-4.)

The Bible, for us the most familiar example of Semitic literature, is simply the highest expression of the intuitive genius of a believing people.

The God of History and the Gods of Nature

Now, therefore, fear the LORD and serve him completely and sincerely. Cast out the gods your fathers served beyond the River and in Egypt, and serve the LORD. If it does not please you to serve the LORD, decide today whom you will serve, the gods your fathers served beyond the River or the gods of the Amorites in whose country you are dwelling. As for me and my household, we will serve the LORD.

(Jos 24:14-15)

The ancient world was a world of many gods. Even "the LORD, your God" of the creed of Deuteronomy 6:25ff was but one God among the many. Though Yahweh was the God of the nation of Israel, practical monotheism (worship/acknowledgement of but one God) was not achieved until a full seven centuries after entry into the promised land—which occurred about 1250 B.C. In the meantime allegiance to the Lord God was not unmixed with an occasional profound bow to the gods of Canaan.

The Hebrew transition from the life of semi-nomads to the sedentary life of farmers in Canaan had far-reaching implications for their understanding of God. Yahweh had been the God of the wanderers; but Israel's new relationship was to the soil. Now her problem was with rainfall, the rotation of the seasons, with fertility—in a word, with the things which were the concern of Canaan's Baal.

Therefore, it is not surprising to read that the Israelites turned to the gods of the land for success in agriculture. In other events, however, especially in war, they would turn to Yahweh. Perhaps the cult of Yahweh was thought of as the official public religion; the other cult as belonging to home and farm life.

In popular worship there was the tendency for the two faiths to intermingle. Such syncretism (the blending of religious beliefs) was common in the Fertile Crescent. But Israel's covenant stated in no uncertain terms, "You shall not have other gods besides me" (Ex 20:3). Yahweh was Lord over all of Israel's life. To juxtapose Yahweh as Lord of history and Baal as lord or master in the area of fertility was a violation of the covenant.

The conflict between Yahweh and Baal is manifested in attitudes toward sex. In Baalism sex was elevated to the divine. Baal had his consort and entered into union with her. Yahweh had no consort. According to the prophets, Israel's God despised the notion of being worshiped in sexual rites. The very thought of the license which such worship encouraged was repulsive to the more perceptive of Israel's thinkers.

In Israel's faith, God's power was revealed in history, in events: in deliverance from slavery, in the gift of a land, in the call to a covenant life. Yahweh was the *living God,* not a fertility god subject to the death and resurrection of the natural world. Baalism taught *control* or manipulation of the gods so as to gain present goods. Israel's faith taught *obedience* and *trust* in God; it called men to a relationship of *love.*

It took generations for the clear-cut emergence of the true strength and uniqueness of the Israelite faith. In the end, Yahweh, who controlled history, won out in the rivalry with the gods who controlled nature.

Study Guide for Chapter 1

Using the Bible as a Key to Ancient Things

1) A complex movement of "clans and languages," "lands and nations" preceded the history of Bible times. Read, or at least scan, Genesis 10, the "Table of the Nations." Then, look at the map on page 22. Note how the biblical author, from the data he has at hand, situates the nations of the world.

2) The Semite spoke of reality in living, graphic, sensual imagery. Read Psalm 23. Be sure to refer to the footnotes in your Bible. What is the psalmist actually portraying? Which are the images used? How might a more technical modern author portray the same theme?

3) The Israelites were familiar with the borrowed imagery from ancient Mesopotamian mythology. Read Genesis 3:24. The mythological notion of creatures half-man and half-animal—cherubim—as guardians of temples

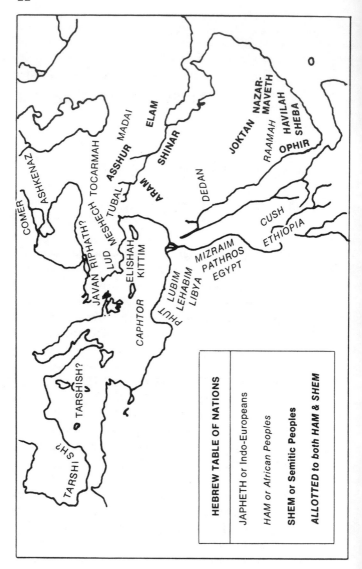

and palaces is used to express Israelite belief that God has sacred ministers. Read Psalms 74:13,14 and 89:11 where certain mythological monsters personify the watery chaos over which God exercises dominion at creation.

4) Parallelism is characteristic of Semitic thought. Read Psalm 67. How many parallel verses/ thoughts are included? Read Psalm 71:1-8. Note the parallel verses.

5) It took generations for Israel to clarify its faith in Yahweh. Read Judges 2:10-19. This tells of the repeated infidelity of early Israel and the constant fidelity of Yahweh to his people.

6) In the end, Yahweh won out in the contest with the gods of nature. Read 2 Maccabees 1:24-25— written sometime after 124 B.C. Note the strength of the faith in the Lord as expressed in this prayer by a much later Jewish people. Here absolute monotheism is without question.

25/75

Still the people remained at a distance, while Moses approached the cloud where God was. The LORD told Moses, "Thus shall you speak to the Israelites: You have seen for yourselves that I have spoken to you from heaven."

Exodus 20:21-22

Chapter 2

The Bible:
A Faith Perspective

Man is a questioner. He questions himself. He questions his universe. Where did I come from? Where am I going? How did the world come about? What is the source of good? Why evil? Is there any hope?

More than 3,000 years ago a new people was brought forth not by political power but by one who identified himself as Yahweh—*he who is always with you.* This new nation, Israel, recognized Yahweh as its creator, its Lord and God. The questions which had always intrigued man were now answered and reanswered in terms of this people's faith in their God.

Their answers were discovered neither in the words of theory nor in those of philosophy, but in flesh-and-blood events. The Israelites recognized Yahweh as present and active in the making of their history.

Brought Forth Within a Believing People

The Jewish Bible. As centuries passed, Israel's faith gave rise to a substantial body of literature—at first oral and later written. Various styles and forms of literature were produced—for example, history, novels, legal codes, poetry, prophecy. These separate literary treasures were later edited and woven together until, as a whole, they became "the book."

The Jewish Bible emerged, then, out of a people very much taken up with the concrete realities of the human situation: with its joys and its tears, its slavery and its freedom, its life and its death. Above all, it was concerned with man in need of salvation, and it manifested the hope of salvation engendered by Yahweh's continued presence with his people in event after event.

The Christian Bible. Jesus was born a Jew and an heir to Judaism's religious traditions. In time, not only many of his contemporaries but people in each generation down to our day recognized that Jesus had been entrusted with the unique and divine mission of fulfilling the Jewish—the human—hope of salvation. Jesus had been ordained as God's complete answer to man's questions about himself and his situation.

Though Jesus suffered death, the lot of all men, his disciples experienced him as raised up by God and established as Lord. As had been the Jewish custom in face of salvation events in the past, the followers of Jesus reflected on this Jesus-event and on all the Jesus-happenings during the years from approximately 4 B.C. to 30 A.D. What Jesus had done and what he had said was remembered and interpreted in light of the fuller faith-understanding which his resurrection and his followers' own new life in the Spirit made possible.

And as had happened before in Jewish history, a new set of traditions began to evolve: the sayings of Jesus and his teaching about the Kingdom, the story of his passion and death, hymns used in celebrations in his memory, formulas expressing faith in Jesus, statements of healings and wonders done in behalf of others, stories of his birth, resurrection accounts. In turn, Jesus was preached about in sermons, written about in letters.

This new set of Jesus traditions was not formed in isolation. Faith in Jesus as Lord and Savior was made possible only because of his recognized continuity with the history of the Jewish people: Jesus was the promised Messiah, the King and Savior which *the book* had heralded. Indeed, he was even more: He was the very Word of the God of Judaism become flesh.

Mark, one of the disciples, early set himself to the task of drawing together the various oral and written data about Jesus. Matthew, Luke and John followed suit, although each had his own added source of information, his own purpose in writing and his own theological insight.

When early Christian housekeeping had been completed, these four Gospels, a volume of 21 letters, a history of the early Church (Acts) and a book called Revelations emerged as the recognized Christian Scriptures. In turn, these were considered as belonging to *the book*. Henceforth, the Bible of the Jews and these recognized (canonical) writings of the Church constituted a new unity, the Christian Bible. Often the Jewish Bible is referred to as the Old Testament, that is, the books of the Old Covenant or Law. The specifically Christian contribution of 27 books is spoken of as the New Testament, or books of the New Covenant or Law.

An Inspired Book

The gift of two believing communities, the Jewish and the early Christian, the Bible is Christianity's most sacred book. The Spirit of God breathed in and upon the men who reflected upon God/man events. He guided them as they interpreted these events and then spoke and/or wrote.

Yet the Spirit did not dictate the text. Rather, each man was his own man; he was a man of his own time. He listened to and was a voice out of his community. He spoke and/or wrote in familiar vocabulary, language, nuances and forms. With an awareness of God's overarching yet closely abiding presence and demands, he discussed the social, economic, political and religious questions pressing upon his community.

Indeed, for the people out of which the Bible emerged, the whole of life was religious. God's domain was unlimited: his power and dominion, his justice and grace covered the earth. He revealed himself in the affairs of man, made known his fatherly will and designs. In time, his Son became

flesh so that as brother he might communicate more
fully and intensely with man. Finally, he sent his
Spirit into the heart of every believer that the
response of man to the revealing God might be a perfect one.

The Norm of Christianity

Christian Doctrine. The Bible, Christianity's most
sacred book, has served as the norm for Christian
thinking down through the centuries. As doctrinal
traditions have crystallized in the Church, it has
been customary to hearken back to the Scriptures—
the writings—to find there the fine root-lines from
which each tradition has grown. It is expected that
all essential doctrines should be found there at least
in embryonic form.

Christian Liturgy. Christianity's central liturgical
act—elaborate though it has become—still basically
derives from worship customs followed in the days
when Christianity was first born: (1) the gathering of
the community; (2) the reading of the Scriptures and
an explanation; (3) the giving of thanks; (4) the eating of the *bread* and the drinking of the *cup* in
remembrance of the Lord Jesus.

Christian Living. An ethical religion, Christianity
still looks to the Bible for the *demands* which its
Founder makes of those who commit themselves to
his *way*.

Christian Teaching. Since the Bible, Christianity's
most sacred book, serves as the norm of Christian

doctrine and conduct and, next to the very person of Jesus himself, is basic to the liturgical act, it must necessarily figure dominantly in the Church's official teaching act: in its *catechesis*. Or, as the majority of us are more readily inclined to say: in its religious instruction.

Source of Mixed Feelings

In this favored position, the Bible is often experienced by many Christians with somewhat the same mixed feelings as God himself is experienced. On the one hand, the sacred book attracts. In its openness—that is, in its clarity of expression, in its *touchableness*—it inspires, invites, arouses awe, commands reverence and respect. On the other hand, that same book causes uneasiness. In its hiddenness—that is, in its expression of life at its depths, in its obscurity, in its *situatedness* in the *long, long ago* and the *far, far away*—it creates questions, arouses a holy fear, disturbs.

Understandably, there is no easy resolution of such mixed feelings in face of the Word of God. Concerned with the God-question and the man-question, the Bible is very much involved in mystery—mystery which God invites us to penetrate and to search.

Because of this call to search, the stance of the devout Christian before Scripture must be a dynamic one. That which is most open and accessible must be reverently unfolded so that its revelatory light may be brought to bear upon human experiences today. That which is obscure and provoking must be approached prayerfully, yes—but also with the insights provided by contemporary studies. Because here, indeed, a wonderful thing is happening in our time. The secular sciences are providing us with new keys to unlock the sacred.

A Book of Truth

Invariably, it is said that the Bible is *truth*. And it is!

What then, for example, about the apparent contradictions between the scientific theories of evolution and the biblical account of God's primordial creative activity? If I hold to the theory of evolution, am I automatically guilty of denying *truth* to the Genesis narrative, or vice versa? Not at all. Actually, both may be held as truth by the believer. The apparent contradiction is readily resolved by a profoundly simple insight: The theory of evolution expresses *a scientific truth;* the Genesis account, on the other hand, expresses *a religious truth,* a faith concept.

The religious truth is this: God is the Creator. All that exists was brought into being by his word, was made by him—heaven and earth, light, firmament, the order of water and earth, vegetation, sun and moon and stars, swimming creatures and winged creatures, beasts and, as a culmination of his creative talents, man made in his image and likeness. This is the religious truth to which both Jews and Christians ascribe.

The Genesis story which tells this truth breaks the creative event up into seven days. This literary device employed by the author to convey the religious truth had its own theological purposes—for example, to reinforce the sanctity of the Sabbath. The author did not share our scientific worldview and was not trying to make a scientific statement.

This is the important thing: In the beginning, *God created*. He is the impetus, the source of all that is. To science may be left the task of divining the scientific truth of *how long ago, in what manner* and *over how long a period*. Then, when science has done its work, surely scientific truth and religious truth will resolve themselves into unity. *Truth* is simple: It originates in the One; it rests ultimately in the One.

In the following chapters we will return more than once to this notion of the Bible as a book of religious truth. Indeed, this is a primary insight. It underwrites still further the task of scholars and scientific students of the Bible. It serves as a firm basis for those of us who look to the Bible for guidance in answering the most profound human questions in this our 20th century.

The Bible and Beyond

1) Take out your Bible.
   a) Find the division between the Old Testament and the New Testament. Note the length of each.
   b) Look at the Table of Contents. Note the number and names of the books in the Old Testament. Note the number and names of the books in the New Testament.

2) The authors of the Old Testament books used different literary forms.
   a) 1 and 2 Chronicles are history books, though a different kind of history than we are used to. Page through 1 Chronicles 9:35—16. Note the section headings.
   b) Ruth is a religious novel. Read Ruth 2:1-16 and see the blossoming of a romance.
   c) The Psalms are hymns or songs. Read Psalm 117, an abbreviated hymn of praise to God.
   d) Jonah is a didactic story—that is, it bears a message. Read this fascinating story. Note

the message: God's mercy reaches out to all people.

3) The Israelites recognized God as present and active in their midst. Out of this faith they eventually fashioned the Bible. Read Psalm 103:1-17. Which are the activities of God praised by the psalmist?

4) The majority of Americans profess belief in the same God praised in Psalm 103. Are we as conscious as the psalmist of God's activity in our world? How do we show this consciousness? What are some signs of our failure to recognize God's activity?

5) Biblical authors made purposeful use of genealogies as a teaching device. Look at Matthew 1:1-17. Note how Matthew cleverly maintains a continuity between the Old Testament and the New Testament. Note in particular verses 16 and 17 which explicitly use the word *messiah*.

6) Pope Pius XII encouraged biblical studies in an encyclical letter (*Divino Afflante Spiritu*) published in 1943. He wrote:
Inspired by the Divine Spirit, the Sacred Writers composed those books, which God, in his paternal charity toward the human race, deigned to bestow on them in order "to teach, to reprove, to correct, to instruct in justice: that the man of God may be perfect, furnished to every good work" (2 Tim 3:16) . . . . Let

the interpreter then, with all care and without neglecting any light derived from recent research, endeavor to determine the peculiar character and circumstances of the sacred writer, the age in which he lived, and sources written or oral to which he had recourse and the forms of expression employed.

How could a better understanding of the message of the Bible help us to be better Christians? Can all our questions, though, be answered by the Bible?

"Abraham, Abraham! ... Do not lay your hand on the boy,"
said the LORD's messenger. "Do not do the least thing to him. I
know now how devoted you are to God, since you did not withhold from me your own beloved son."

Genesis 22:11-12

Chapter 3

The Bible: Story of Salvation

As far back as man could project in history, reaching even into the realms of prehistory, he had recognized his helplessness. Examining the past, looking at the present, peering into the future, the people of Israel recognized that man was fully man only when he lived in relationship with the Lord God.

God had created man. God had persisted with him and even promised blessings despite his failures. God alone could and would bring him to salvation, to his full potential, and this through an ongoing act of newly creative and salvific love.

Christians, in turn, assented to the insights of their religious ancestors, saw them carried to fullness in Jesus Christ, and looked forward toward a future where all would be consummated—completed, perfected—and in unity with God.

Thus the Bible became from beginning to end the story of salvation—the many-faceted narrative of man as he journeys through life nurtured, watched over, supported, invited but never forced, purified through punishment/suffering yet always forgiven, free though still responsible, lost but always redeemed anew by his Savior God.

It is this long, colorful, oftentimes painful human history which we plan to explore through the pages of the Bible: the story of salvation. While our chief concern here is the Old Testament, we will, as in Chapter 2, carry the salvation story forward into the New Testament and even into our own times.

Genesis: Mankind in General

Man in God. The Bible offers the reader two accounts of the creation of man. Both were put in written form long after the Exodus and the Sinai experience through which the Israelites became conscious that they were God's chosen people. Both represent Israel's faith assertion in the face of her many pagan neighbors that the Lord God is the author of man's existence.

The earlier account (about 950 B.C.) begins with Genesis 2:7: "The Lord God formed man out of the clay of the ground and blew into his nostrils the breath of life, and so man became a living being."

There is something *earthy* about man: Formed with care "out of the clay of the ground," he has a close kinship to the earth. There is also something of *spirit* about man: The breath of life blown into his nostrils by the Lord God made this clay a living being. The remainder of Genesis 2 tells us much about man: He is called to obedience by God—"Do not eat"—something which presupposes man-in-relationship. He is called to society—"It is not good for man to be alone."

The second creation account, placed now in Genesis 1, was committed to writing as much as 400 years after the first by a member of the priestly family. But, in *oral* form, it could well be the older of the two. Obviously, this report represents insights into the story of man's origin—insights granted by Spirit-guided observation of man in his world:

> God created man in his image; in the divine image he created him; male and female he created them. God blessed them, saying: "Be fertile and multiply; fill the earth and subdue it. Have dominion . . . ." God looked at everything he had made, and he found it very good.
>
> (Gn 1:27-31)

Thus was creation at its onset: nature, beast, man and God enjoying a time of perfect harmony. "He found it very good." A grace-full situation, indeed!

Man in a State of Fallenness. The Israelites were aware, however, that another element had entered into man's situation: sin and evil, an ought-not-to-be-ness. Somehow, someway, man's natural neediness as creature had given way to a sense of lostness, of fallenness, of purposelessness. The story of Adam, a tale of disobedience, is Israel's attempt to dramatize mankind's fall from original harmony. We shall look more closely at this story in Chapter 5.

But the fall did not mean that our first ancestors

experienced a sense of *total* abandonment by God. Eve exclaims at the birth of Cain, "I have produced a man with the help of the Lord" (Gn 4:1). And other references in Genesis 4 through 11 likewise testify to an experience of the ongoing activity of God in the world. Nonetheless, biblical authors were convinced of man's situation of helplessness; a more direct and particular intervention into human affairs was demanded if we were ever to experience an at-one-ness with the world and our God again.

The Patriarchs: Men Chosen From the Many

Though the centuries-later experience at Mount Sinai was formative of the Israelites as a people, they chose to begin their religious history with the telling of a much earlier event: the call of Abraham.

From amongst all living men the Israelites believed that God had singled out Abraham (Abram) so that the divine purpose of bringing mankind—indeed, all creation—to fulfillment might be newly initiated. This man's loins contained the seed of fresh hope. In a very special sense, Abraham was "patriarch"—first father—in the new order of salvation.

Abraham and his wife, Sarah, emerged out of Mesopotamia, a fertile land, polytheistic in culture, a busy land with its cities resounding to the feet of merchants and traders from far and near. According to the Bible, Abraham was a well-to-do semi-nomad with extensive flocks and a retinue of men or servants to tend them. Somewhere in his career his people had migrated from the fringes of the city of Ur on the Euphrates River to the outskirts of a more north-

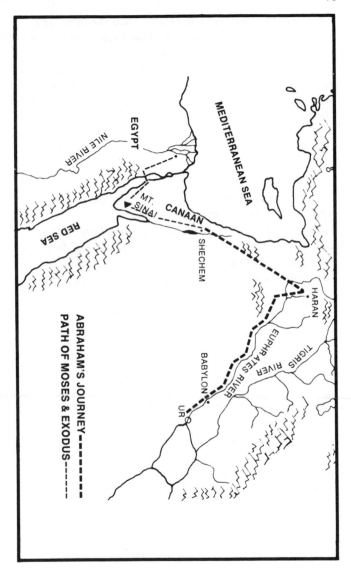

westerly city, Haran (Gn 11:31). (See the map on p. 41.) Eventually he and his clan found their way southward to the land of Canaan.

Actually, Abraham's movement into Canaan represented but a tiny fraction of the migration of semi-nomads which peopled the land anew early in the 20th century B.C. Somewhere in the migration, could we see clearly enough, we would discern the clans of the two other biblical patriarchs, Isaac and Jacob.

Historically these clans of Abraham, Isaac and Jacob were separate clans. For theological reasons, when the traditions grouped about each were finally edited by the priests (400 B.C.), Abraham was set down as the head, the first father of believers. In this position—Abraham, Isaac, Jacob—the stories of the patriarchs have been made to form a prologue to the history of salvation.

As was customary among his contemporaries, Abraham worshiped the patron deity of his family: *El Shaddai,* referred to in later generations as "the God of Abraham" (Ex 3:6). Isaac and Jacob likewise invoked a family or tribal god. Isaac's "El" (i.e., god) was designated as "the Awesome One of Isaac" (Gn 31:42,52); Jacob's as "the Mighty One of Jacob" (Gn 49:24).

Scholars who have familiarized themselves with Ancient Near East patterns of movement and customs say that the biblical stories of Abraham, Isaac and Jacob reflect well the period of history in which they are set, 2000-1700 B.C. These stories represent traditions passed down by word of mouth from generation to generation. And though it cannot be proven that the separate incidents happened exactly as narrated in the written form, neither is there evidence to the contrary. For information about Abraham, Isaac and Jacob we are entirely dependent upon the Bible.

Interestingly enough, incidents in the Genesis story which raise questions for modern readers can be explained in the light of customs of the second millennium B.C. Ancient documents excavated in the 20th century give access to this information.

For example, Abraham's fear that, since he was childless, his steward Eliezer would be the heir (Gn 15:2) is understandable given slave adoption practices at Nuzi in the East-Tigris region (excavated between 1925 and 1931 A.D.). There a couple without children would adopt a slave who acted as servant while they lived and inherited on their death.

Likewise, customs at Nuzi explain why Jacob's wife, Rachel, stole the household "gods" from her father, Laban (Gn 31:25ff). Possession of these "gods" was tantamount to the right of inheritance.

Scholars are also of the opinion that the body of stories which the ancient tradition has attached to each of the patriarchs went through a long process of assimilation. When the various clans of Abraham, Isaac and Jacob entered Canaan, the original inhabitants already worshiped their own gods at established shrines. These shrines attracted large crowds at festival times. Within their orbit came worship, marketing, buying and selling, the settlement of differences, courting and betrothal.

Newcomers were quite naturally caught up in this customary rhythm of life. And so it is not surprising to find clans which claimed the God of Abraham, the God of Isaac, or the God of Jacob frequenting the same shrines as the earlier natives. Indeed, these new arrivals even celebrated their own cultic festivals there. Unconsciously, each clan merged the oral story of its founder with the legends of the founders of Canaanite cults. For example, one clan which worshiped the God of Abraham centered itself at the tree sanctuary of Mamre. They made this shrine's cultic saga of three heavenly visitors their own by relating the visit to their own patriarch, Abraham (Gn 18:1-15).

It was this type of material which early Israel gathered and shaped into a kind of epic of the ancestors. Later still, but before the monarchy (about 1000 B.C.), this was linked with the traditions of the exodus, Sinai, and the conquest of the land to form a grand epic of the origin of Israel.

Evidence internal to the Bible gives reason to believe that this narrative of origins continued to develop but along *separate* lines in southern Judah and northern Israel (thus, the Yahwist and the Elohist traditions). Eventually, possibly after 721 B.C., the two separate strands or traditions were edited into a single narrative. As already noted, later editions, notably one done by the priests around 400 B.C., place the three patriarchs on a chronological time line as father, son and grandson. This brought further fusion to what had originally been separate units or cycles of tradition (see Gn 12—50).

God's Invitation; Abraham's Response. The key to the Abraham event and even to the interpretation of the entire religious experience of the Jews is found in Genesis 12:1-4a ("The LORD said to Abram: 'Go forth . . . .' Abram went as the LORD directed him"). What the sacred writer has done in these few lines is typical of much biblical reporting: Years of history may be telescoped into a single episode.

In actuality, scholars believe that the settlement of Abraham and his clan in the heart of the land of Canaan, the Promised Land, was preceded by periods of seasonal movement in and out of the territory—a practice to which the Canaanites were not hostile. During the growing season Abraham's semi-nomadic clan had been accustomed to crossing over to the outskirts of the more fertile land of the Canaanites and planting crops. Following the harvest and with the onset of the dry season, they gathered up their families and belongings and departed with their flocks to more verdant grazing areas beyond Canaan. But, on some noteworthy occasion the pattern of moving in and out was broken and the clan penetrated the land and went about it, in its length and breadth, as if it were their own.

The permanent dwelling of Abraham in Canaan was not viewed as a chance event. Rather, it had been precipitated by a call issued by the God of Abraham. The tradition of this call and the ensuing promises of possession of the land and a great posterity goes back to the time of the patriarchs themselves and remained substantially unchanged. Abraham was—both for his immediate clan as well as for the later Israelites—the recipient of the primordial revelation which shaped destinies and grounded faith for all generations. "The LORD said to Abram: 'Go forth from the land of your kinsfolk and from your father's house to a land that I will show you' " (Gn 12:1).

Move, man! Have the courage to place one foot in front of the other. Do something about your situation. I, your God, will be there *giving* to you. The initiative is mine; the response is yours. The faith dimension of the patriarch—the first father—is highlighted in pregnant words: "Abram went as the LORD directed him" (Gn 12:4).

We likewise hear the divine call urging us to *move*. Believing, we must proceed to translate the received word into human activity, to respond dynamically, to be about salvation things, to move with hope into an oftentimes unknown and uncertain future.

The Election of the One for the Many. The call of Abraham and the promise which followed were not for his personal benefit alone. The Israelites believed that this one man had been chosen from all of mankind so that he *and they*—his posterity by birth or by faith in Yahweh—might be the bearers of good things for all the nations. Indeed, this was their vocation.

In this understanding of their call and the promise of blessings for "all the communities of the earth," the Israelites expressed their faith that all is not absurd or meaningless: Universal history has been seeded with hope. These words of Yahweh are few but the import is far-reaching:

> "I will make of you a great nation, and I will bless you;
>
> I will make your name great, so that you will be a blessing . . . .
>
> All the communities of the earth shall find blessing in you." (Gn 12:2-3)

But even Abraham twice challenges the initiative of the Lord God in his affairs. (Read Genesis 15, its footnotes and other references.) His first difficulty has to do with an heir: "O Lord GOD, what good will your gifts be, if I keep on being childless . . .?" (Gn 15:2). The Lord's answer: "Look up at the sky and count the stars, if you can. Just so . . . shall your descendants be" (Gn 15:5). Abraham's faith response is a decisive act for himself as well as for all those who in subsequent generations will call him "father" (of believers): "Abraham put his faith in the LORD, who credited it to him as an act of righteousness" (Gn 15:6).

Abraham's second question is about the promised land. "O Lord GOD . . . how am I to know that I shall possess it?" (Gn 15:8).

With infinite patience the Lord responds by setting up a solemn covenant with the patriarch to place the divine seal upon the promise. This tradition of covenant belongs to the Abraham body of stories and was later assimilated by the Israelites. Believing that the Abraham event extended into their own history, they retold the original story and cleverly included in it a synopsis or creedal statement of that history (Gn 15:13-16).[1]

The Promise Continued in Isaac and Jacob. The ques-

1. In much the same way as we Christians recite our Creed in the solemn liturgical act of the Mass, so did the Israelites recite their summary faith-statements when they recalled their history and celebrated God's mighty deeds. In including these in their book of saving history, the Bible, they set them within specific events, as is evidenced in this chapter describing the covenant with Abraham.

tion of whether or not Isaac and Jacob were, in fact, direct descendants of Abraham misses the impact of the religious truth conveyed by the priestly editors: God willed to carry forth his plan of salvation through the father of believers, Abraham. To reinforce this theology, the authors tell how Isaac, in his turn, was chosen over his half-brother, Ismael (Gn 26:3-5). And of the sons of Isaac, Jacob became the elected and specified bearer of the promise (Gn 28:13-15).

It should be remarked that Abraham, Isaac and Jacob were, indeed, inheritors of the promises and their fulfillment *even in their own day*. For instance, Abraham is noted as buying a family burying ground at Hebron (Gn 23). Thereby he became a landholder and one of the men of Hebron. Time, nonetheless, brought a further unfolding and subsequent fulfillment of these same promises in succeeding generations, notably at the period of the conquest of Canaan and during the reign of David.

The Development of the Salvation Narrative. The Abraham-Isaac-Jacob events were not treated with cold objectivity by our Bible people. Neither were the stories put immediately into a once-for-all form by one author. Worked and reworked, told and retold by generation after generation of Israelites, the eventually-fixed narratives of the patriarchs reflect later as well as earlier history. This is particularly true of the promise passages in Genesis 12:1-3, as already noted, as well as those in Genesis 26:3-5 and 28:13-15. In their fixed form, these key verses hold, in embryo, the tale of God-Israel relationships over many centuries.

Truly, the promises spoken as much as eight centuries earlier had been fulfilled. Israel's writers of a much later generation could affirm this as, in retrospect, they fashioned a dialogue between God and each of the patriarchs. Land, a numerous posterity, and blessing for themselves and others had come to the patriarchs. But the sweep of God's will to save had been broadened as time passed to embrace succeeding generations no matter where they spread.

Quite consciously, therefore, the sacred writers brought all Israel—past, present, future—as well as "the nations" under the scope of God's promises. Thus, Israelites of the ninth century B.C. could easily celebrate their present inheritance in the dramatic reenactment of God's dialogue with Jacob:

"I, the LORD, am the God of your forefather Abraham and the God of Isaac; the land on which you are lying I will give to you and your descendants. These shall be as plentiful as the dust of the earth, and through them you shall spread out east and west, north and south. In you and your descendants all the nations of the earth shall find blessing." (Gn 28:13,14)

Israel: A People Chosen From the Nations

To this day Jews celebrate the Mount Sinai event as the decisive experience in their history. Sinai was the primordial event in the history of Israel's faith, and remained the rallying point of their faith in several ways:

1) The Sinai experience was the focus through which Israel gained perspective on its own past history and the prehistory of the world; through

which Israel continued to discover God's revelation in its present; and through which Israel maintained the vision to approach the future with hope.

2) Sinai was the force which, over the centuries, drew together peoples from various tribes and traditions and formed them into the larger community of Israel.

3) Sinai was the event whose liturgical celebration made present to each new generation the experience of the exodus of the people of God: the flight from Egypt, the passage through the Red Sea, the sojourn in the desert, the entry and establishment in the land of Canaan. In a word, Sinai was the pivotal event which held within itself the entire story of a people's passover from slavery in a foreign land to covenant union with the Lord in a land of their own.

The People Chosen. It was a rather motley group of ex-slaves, however, which underwent the transforming event at the Mount. Brought down to Egypt, a foreign land, four centuries earlier by a famine, the Hebrews were favored at first only to have their posterity reduced to helpless and cruel slavery. Led by Moses, they had finally, around 1280 B.C., escaped from Egypt and repaired to the area of the Sinai desert.

The Sinai Experience. It was at the base of Mount Sinai that the Lord God bound this chosen people to himself in solemn covenant action. We are completely dependent upon the Jewish Scriptures for the record of what has come to be known as the Sinai experience. The narrative, as contained in Exodus 19,

20 and 24, was put in its present form in the fifth century B.C., although the author employed written sources from the ninth and eighth century B.C. It is a faith report rather than a purely objective recital. That is, it is a human attempt to articulate what happened when that group of refugees bowed down in allegiance before Yahweh, the Lord, whom they were able to identify with El, the God of Abraham (Ex 3:13,16ff).[2] It is an attempt to concretize, to make visual, one of the most profound and far-reaching experiences of a people.

Awed by the graciousness and might of Yahweh in the face of their own frailty and smallness, they knew their God as saying: "I bore you up on eagle wings and brought you here to myself" (Ex 19:4). They described their sense of *election* and *call to covenant* in these words: "Therefore, if you hearken to my voice and keep my covenant, you shall be my special possesssion, dearer to me than all other people, though all the earth is mine" (Ex 19:5).

Their sense of *mission* was expressed in language which has challenged the nobility and generosity of

---

2. Historians of religion say that pre-Mosaic ancestors of Israel preserved the memory that they had not always worshiped Yahweh. His self-revelation only entered their lives at a definite time (Ex 3 and 6). Two of the biblical traditions designate the God of the patriarchs as El or Elohim (God)— and use Yahweh only after Exodus 3 and 6. But the author of Genesis 2:4[b]ff uses Yahweh Elohim, Lord God, right from the beginning. However, several hundred years elapsed between the revelation of Yahweh at Sinai and the writing of this tradition with its unique theological purpose. In the meantime much lived dialogue had passed between worshipers of the ancestral God (El/Elohim) and the small Jacob group which had entered the land following Sinai.

every son of Israel to this day: "You shall be to me a kingdom of priests, a holy nation" (Ex 19:6).

Their *response* to the terms of the covenant brought to them from God by Moses was this: "Everything the LORD has said, we will do" (Ex 19:8).

Their celebration of this unique God-and-man encounter took the form of a covenant ceremony (Ex 24:3-8). They thereby signed and sealed a sacred agreement between Yahweh and themselves forever.

The Sinai Experience Made Present in Every Generation. Though but a core group of the people later known as Israelites underwent the transforming experience of Mount Sinai, their posterity by the millions have participated in the event. This is made possible by liturgical celebration in which past events are remembered and made present in sacred word and action.

Christians can look to the Mass as an analogy. In the Eucharistic celebration—in word and act—we continually make present and participate in the saving life-death-resurrection-glorification of Jesus. So the people of Israel through covenant renewal celebration make the Sinai experience available to each generation.

Thus, each succeeding generation of Israelites knew itself as present at Mount Sinai. This included Israelites by birth as well as the people who joined them by alliance and acceptance of Yahweh.

The faith conviction that theirs was a history of salvation for themselves as well as for the world dominated Israelite thought down through the centuries. In expression and development, this conviction went through successive stages and assumed many facets not always consistent or easy to sort out.

Two ideas that eventually gained prominence were these: that a messianic king—the offspring of the great King David—would serve as the instrument through whom Yahweh would fulfill the destiny of Israel (read Psalm 89); that Mount Zion, the seat of the Temple, would be the center from which God's redeeming activity would radiate.

The power of their faith conviction enabled this people to recognize in their triumph or vicissitude, in their might or weakness, God's creative or re-creative activity. Some of their most sublime reflections are expressed in Isaiah 24-27. Indeed, even though Israel might fail in its mission, God's will to salvation would not, could not fail:

On this mountain the LORD of hosts
will provide for all peoples
A feast of rich food and choice wines,
juicy, rich food and pure, choice wines.
On this mountain he will destroy
the veil that veils all peoples,
The web that is woven over all nations;
he will destroy death forever.
The Lord GOD will wipe away
the tears from all faces;
The reproach of his people he will remove
from the whole earth; for the LORD has
spoken. (Is 25:6-8)

Jesus: One Chosen for the Salvation of All

More than 18 centuries elapsed from the election of Abraham until the historical election of Jesus.

Chosen from among the Jewish people—a remnant of the once numerous and powerful Israelite people—Jesus, like Abraham, like Israel, was elected for the salvation of the many. Jesus summed up the salvation hopes and the salvific mission of Israel. Apostolic Christianity saw him in his uniqueness as Messiah, King, Lord, the bearer of salvation within his very person. Indeed, Jesus was the servant, the one on whom the favor of the Lord rested and the one who would bring forth justice to the nations. (Compare Isaiah 42:1, 6 with Luke 3:21, 22.)

Following his baptism—the moment of his call—Jesus began to proclaim the messianic kingdom (Mt 4:17) and to set his hand to its task. His task is revealed in his message to John the Baptizer: ". . . the blind recover their sight, cripples walk, lepers are cured, the deaf hear, dead men are raised to life, and the poor have the good news preached to them" (Mt 11:5).

Standing within the faith of his ancestors, Jesus gave sign that salvation is *of this world,* that it has to do with fulfilling man's needs and remedying his sinful situation. In his own person, Jesus extended the boundaries of the Abrahamic promises—of land and posterity and earthly blessings—and of the later Jewish notion of a new earth.

Living in total openness to the Spirit, Jesus daily narrowed the distance which the first man had put between himself and God. Finally, embracing even death, choosing the will of the Father to the end, Jesus burst through into a glorious and new life. In this final thrust forward, Jesus, through his solidarity with all his human brothers and sisters, retrieved all humanity—indeed, all creation—from its fallenness. Salvation was accomplished.

Christians: Men Called for Others

It is now nearly 2,000 years since the election of Jesus as the redeemer of humanity. But the process of election continues. It continues each time a person prompted by the Spirit in Baptism assumes the position of *son* in identification with Jesus Christ, the perfectly open and obedient Son of God. In this Christic role, the Christian, like all others in the long historical line dating from Abraham, is called in oneness with his community to be *for* others. Thus the salvation event already accomplished in Christ will be realized within individuals as well as within their communities.

Study Guide for Chapter 3

Salvation in Israel and Beyond

1) The first five books of the Bible are actually four separate strands of traditions edited together in stages until they reached their present form about 400 B.C. Each tradition grew up within a particular section of Palestine (earlier Canaan). This is the theory of Bible critics:

   • The Yahwist tradition arose in the south, Judah, and from an environment very close to the court (about 950 B.C.).

   • The Elohist tradition, distinguished especially by its use of *Elohim* for God, arose in the north, Israel (about 850 B.C.).

   • The Deuteronomic tradition, dealing mostly with Moses and law, grew up around shrines in the north but was brought to Judah and put in its final form (about 650 B.C. and later).

   • The Priestly tradition was the product of the south (about 550 B.C. and later). It has to do with worship concerns.

a) Read Genesis 2 from verse 4 to the end—the Yahwist creation story. The Lord God *formed man,* that is, he made man with care and attention. Could the biblical author be trying to say something special about man? How does he indicate man's call to live in relationship? How does this show an openness to growth on the part of man?

b) Read Genesis 1:26—2:4, the Priestly creation story. From the two accounts, draw up a word description of primitive man's spiritual condition.

2) Genesis 3 tells us of a rupture in the God-man relationship. Read Genesis 3:15 and its footnote. What does this first bit of "good news" say to Christians?

3) Read Genesis 12:1-4a. Point out the following elements denoting the God-Abram relationship: the one who speaks first; the one who invites; the one elected; the promises; the response of man. Note the new openness, the new closeness to God as opposed to the distance of Adam. Why do we trace *new hope* for all men back to Abram?

4) God invited Abram to *move* and Abram *did move.* How does God still speak to each of us and invite us to move, to give up a less worthy way of life, to grow as humans should grow? Would you consider this also to be a "call to salvation"? Why?

5) The Israelites believed that God was involved in the making of history. Read Genesis 15. By promise, in how many saving events will God be involved? Can you point out evidence of "hindsight" in the way the story is presented?

6) The salvation plan of God was worked out in history. Read the promises of the Lord to Isaac (Gn 26:3-5) and to Jacob (Gn 28:13-15; Gn 35:11, 12). Note the similarity of these promises to those made to Abraham. Through such repetition Israel affirmed its faith that God was steadfastly faithful to his original promises.

7) Read Exodus 19 and 24, which constitute a single event. Which are the words of election? Which words indicate Israel's openness to live in relationship with the Lord?

8) Later generations of Israel participated in the salvation events (for example, freedom from slavery, the covenant at Sinai, possession of the promised land) by celebrating them in liturgy. Read Psalm 105:1-11, 44-45. Note the invitation to the congregation to sing to the Lord, to celebrate salvation events.

9) Israel later centralized its liturgy on Mount Zion in Jerusalem. Read Isaiah 25. What do these Israelites consider as belonging to future salvation? What is your reaction to the faith of these people?

The seventh time around ... Joshua said to the people, "Now shout, for the LORD has given you the city and everything in it." ... As the horns blew, ... they raised a tremendous shout. The wall collapsed, and the people stormed the city ... and took it.

Joshua 6:16, 17, 20

Chapter 4

Filling In
Old Testament
Salvation Events

The scope of Israelite history reflected in the Bible covers some 1,700 years, more or less. This chapter takes a panoramic view of this history from the time of Joseph—about 1750 B.C.—to the emergence of Judaism in the fifth century B.C.

Joseph: Bridge in the Tradition

The Joseph story is an independent narrative *later* used to explain the presence of Hebrews in Egypt. It bridges a gap of 400 years—between the patriarchs in Canaan and the Hebrews in Egypt.

It originally circulated as a piece of edifying fiction in northern Israel (although an historical basis for the story is probable). Specifically, it affirms that affairs rest neither in the evil scheming of men nor in the economic situation (the reason for Jacob's move from Canaan to Egypt), but in the hands of God. And though the story itself contains no repetition of the promises made to Abraham, its present position in the Bible indicates the author has carefully related it to the complete epic of salvation.

In brief, Joseph, a young and god-fearing son of the patriarch, Jacob, was sold by his jealous brothers to slave traders and carried to Egypt where he rose to power second only to Pharaoh. In a time of famine in Canaan, he welcomed his father and brothers to Egypt, forgave the brothers, cared for their needs, and settled them by the favor of the Pharaoh in Goshen.

The figure of Joseph has been the focus for some pious creations as well as for several legends. For example, Genesis 39 definitely has a counterpart in the Egyptian "Story of Two Brothers" in which the same theme appears. In the Egyptian story a man resists his older brother's wife who attempts to seduce him. Offended, she falsely accuses him, and her husband then attempts to destroy the younger brother.

The narrative might also reflect a later addition of wisdom literature. (See Chapter 8 of this book.) For example, the story of the relations of Joseph and his brothers culminates with the sublime reflections that all human life is under divine sway: "Even though you meant harm to me, God meant it for good, to achieve his present end, the survival of many people" (Gn 50:20).

To the descendants of the patriarch Jacob—as reflected in the Joseph story—surely belongs the tradition of the Egyptian sojourn and the Exodus.

The time of the migration of these Jacob people[1] to Egypt coincided with the rule of the Hyksos. This was an Asiatic group of Semites who began invading Egypt somewhere around 1720 B.C. Joseph, a foreigner come to power presumably among foreigners, was in a position to favor his people. The expulsion of the Hyksos in 1580 B.C., however, brought a reversal of fortune to the Hebrews: forced labor, cruel slavery (see Ex 1).

Moses: The Man and the Message

Moses was Israel's inspiration and founder. Commissioned by Yahweh as a kind of prophet to his people in Egypt and as his spokesman to Pharaoh, Moses was the great personality behind the Exodus—the going out of the Hebrews (or Israelites) from Egypt. Moses mediated the covenant at Sinai. He laid down Yahweh's commandments. He led the people through every danger from Sinai to Moab.

Around these historical events various traditions developed which underwent centuries of oral transmission, selection, expansion and interpretation. The final editing together of the various Mosaic traditions came as late as the fourth century B.C.

Moses, despite his position as founder of Israel, is not an historical figure in the same sense as David or Solomon, whose personal histories can be reconstructed with a measure of certitude from the biblical narratives. So overwhelming and pervasive

---

1. For the sake of simplicity, "Jacob people" is used in this book. Some writers prefer to be more specific and use "Joseph people."

is the enduring influence of Moses, that the four literary traditions each develop his role in a distinctive manner. For example, in the Yahwist tradition Moses is an inspired shepherd sent to make the Lord's will known (Ex 7:16; 8:16; 9:13). In the Elohist tradition, Israel's theologians present him as God's instrument in effecting deliverance (Ex 3:10,12). He is now a wonder worker—almost a magician (Ex 4:17; 14:16), a prophet (Dt 34:10), and acts as a priest (Ex 24:6).

Noting the literary license of the authors of the separate traditions is not an invitation to deny the existence of Moses. But it does help us to understand why there are details in the Bible that are not grounded historically. A notable example is the story of the infant Moses found in the reeds on the river bank (Ex 2:1ff). This story was probably composed in imitation of a Mesopotamian legend. Egyptians, as far as we know, never practiced infanticide.

The unique quality of Moses was his knowledge of and intimacy with Yahweh who came to be known by the Israelites as Creator, Savior, Judge and Lord of History. Moses's initial encounter with Yahweh is cast in the revelatory drama at Mount Horeb.[2]

"Moses! Moses!" the voice called from the burning bush (Ex 3:4).

The subject of this interpersonal encounter is described as involved in human affairs: "I have *witnessed* the affliction of my people in Egypt and have

2. The reader must be careful to keep in mind that this final form of the burning bush episode depicts a more fully developed faith than would have been possible when the original encounter between Moses and Yahweh occurred many centuries before.

heard their cry of complaint against their slave drivers, so I *know* well what they are suffering" (Ex 3:7; emphases added).

The salvation which this God planned was to be his own doing: "I have come down to rescue them from the hands of the Egyptians" (Ex 3:8). Nonetheless, the people had to cooperate. God had come "to lead them out of that land into a good and spacious land," but he would not pick them up from one land and set them down in another. He would go before them, gracing them with his presence, but they had to follow. When Moses hesitated to act as mediator and leader, God's response was reassuring: "I will be with you" (Ex 3:12).

This God who chose to communicate with his people through Moses was not a strange God. Rather, he was identical with the God of the patriarchs. Moses was directed to tell his people: "The LORD, the God of your fathers, the God of Abraham, the God of Isaac, the God of Jacob" (Ex 3:15), ". . . I AM sent me to you" (Ex 3:14). This, indeed, was *Yahweh,* the God who transcended time and space: *he who is always with you.*

Exodus: People on the Way

The narrative of the final days of the Hebrews in Egypt as given in Exodus is a complex one. Composed by an editor who, in all but a few verses, used existing traditions, it serves basically to express the theology that without Yahweh the situation would have been hopeless. Only his mighty hand was powerful enough to wrest them from the obstinate grasp of Pharaoh. Even natural phenomena—such as hail storms, an unusual darkness or the havoc of locusts—which brought suffering upon the Egyptians and instilled fear were interpreted as expressly the work of God (see Ex 7:14—11).

The Passover Celebration. In origin the Passover ritual stems from a rite practiced by herders. In the spring a young animal was sacrificed in order to secure fertility and prosperity for the flock. Blood was poured on the tent poles (and in later, more settled conditions, on the stiles of the door) to drive away evil powers.

Invested with new meaning—that is, the celebration of God's goodness to Israel—the Passover became a feast sacred to the people of Yahweh. Exodus 12—with no attempt to indicate the centuries of historical development—draws past, present and future into one intense unit: the first Passover of Moses and the highly ritualized Passover celebration through which future generations continued to participate in the same event.

The Miracles. The exodus of the Hebrew slaves, an undertaking spearheaded by Moses, was probably carried out by small groups making their escape during the first half of the 13th century. In the tradition, however, it assumes the proportions of a once-for-all spectacle or chorale, the purpose of which was the confession of theological truth: *Yahweh delivered his people from Egypt.* The site of the biblical "Red Sea" is still undetermined, but the crossing of waters— with its natural symbolism of death and new life—is strongly imbedded in the traditions. (To get an idea of the many different forms this one tradition took, read Ex 14:21-22, Wis 10:18 and also Ps 78:13; 136:13; 114:3.)

The fidelity of Israel's God remained constant and consistent. During the entire desert sojourn the people were able, by Yahweh's providence, to secure sufficient food and drink—a marvel worth retelling for future generations! Storytellers captured the whole of this 40-year-long miracle in two tight episodes: "The Quail and Manna" and "Water From the Rock" (Ex 16—17).

Sinai: Covenant With the Lord. A particular band of Jacob people led by Moses shared the chain of events known as the Exodus, including entry into the covenant with Yahweh at Sinai. After this nucleus penetrated the promised land, they settled down and fused with indigenous peoples to eventually form the nation of Israel. Instead of maintaining a unique group whose ancestors had been present at Mount Sinai, the Israelites universalized the Exodus to the whole people. In other words, henceforth, it was as though each and every future Israelite had come out of Egypt and had stood at the foot of the mountain where Israel's covenant relationship with Yahweh had been first struck up.

It would be a mistake to consider the description of the experience in Exodus 19, 20 and 24 as an objective report. What we have in these chapters is surely based on a solid tradition of how Israel was uniquely set apart from other peoples. In its present form, however, this material has all the earmarks of having been edited or adapted for liturgical use. Through a liturgical reenactment of Sinai, the binding of a people was relived by each new generation.

Chapters 19 and 20 form a kind of "liturgy of the Word"—the story of the Sinai event with its theological interpretation as it was read or chanted in the liturgy. (Consider the liturgy of the Word in our Mass as a parallel.) Chapter 24 describes a covenant ceremony involving a twofold ritual: 1) the sacrifice of animals to Yahweh and the signing or sealing of the covenant with the blood of the victim; 2) the eating of a meal, a good example of a very primitive communion sacrifice.

The animals offered stood for the lives of the participants. The blood sprinkled on the altar and on the people signified the familial or blood relationship established that day with the Lord and with one another. The sharing of a meal of which the principal food was the victim offered to and accepted by God symbolized the sharing in divine life made possible under the covenant.

Sinai: Ten Words of the Lord. Yahweh had initiated the covenant. He had made this people his own: "You shall be my special possession" (Ex 19:5). Now, he speaks to his people in a manner unique in the ancient world—that is, Yahweh is apodictic. He states no conditions. There are no ifs, ands or buts as in other existing codes. Incisely he commands: "You shall not have other gods beside me, . . . you shall not kill, . . . you shall not commit adultery . . ." (Ex 20:3-17).

Watching over the humanity of man in a most elementary fashion, the ten imperatives indicate that allegiance to Yahweh demands the avoidance of certain things that displease him. Like a great net descending upon his chosen people, the will of Yahweh sets them apart as his special possession.

Never spoken of in the Old Testament as the Ten Commandments, these *ten words,* originally all negative in character, confronted each generation and its particular problems with the Lord's will to justice. As centuries passed, Israel's ear became keener and a positive content took over the place of the original negative third and fourth *words.* Thus, these two words now read, respectively: "Remember to keep holy the Lord's day" and "Honor your father and your mother." Later history brought an inner motive for keeping the precepts: Israel is obedient out of love and gratitude to Yahweh.

Joshua and the Conquest

In the course of the 40 years which elapsed between the exodus from Egypt and the entry into the Promised Land, Moses and those who had come with him out of Egypt died. Meanwhile, faith in Yahweh was nurtured in a new generation. This generation, under the leadership of Joshua, succeeded in penetrating and securing a strong foothold in the hand of Canaan, a territory which, to recent desert-dwellers, was surely a land "flowing with milk and honey."

The story is told in epic form in the book of Joshua. In true epic fashion Joshua is the conquering hero before whom all difficulties fade. The theological intent in using this literary form is obvious: Israel's God is mighty; he has a plan of salvation. No one can thwart his will to have his people occupy the land.

In contrast to the Joshua account, other biblical

sources as well as archeological findings make clear the fact that the conquest of Canaan by the Israelites in the 13th century B.C. was anything but immediate. For example, Judges 1:1—2:5 narrates how certain tribes could but slowly infiltrate territory assigned them. Some could do no more than live alongside the native peoples before becoming gradually strong enough to subdue them. The conquest was accompanied by great destruction and upheaval. On the other hand, many of the Canaanites were not hostile and readily allied themselves with the newcomers, some even recognizing an ancient and distant kinship.

Joshua 24 tells how this leader gathered together all the tribes of Israel at Shechem for a covenant renewal ceremony. In solemn celebration a tribal confederacy or alliance was formed and all members, having chosen Yahweh over other gods, committed themselves to "serve the Lord, the God of Israel" and "obey his voice." (See Jos 24.)

Events in the Promised Land

Judges. For several centuries following the conquest, the Israelites led the simple life of village farmers. Their unity lay in the worship of Yahweh and in a common tribal feeling. There was no strong political system. Indications are that judges (referred to by historians as *lesser* judges) administered justice at stations up and down the land (see Jgs 1-5).

Another order of judges existed as well. Whenever the rights of a particular tribe were threatened by an outsider, Yahweh anointed a leader (a judge) to vindicate his people. In each instance the anointed and spirit-filled one rose above his ordinary human limitations, accomplished his task, and then went into rapid decline. So went the course of the careers of charismatic persons like Samson and Gideon. (Read Jgs 8:24-27 which speaks of "the ruin of Gideon and his family.")

Kings: Old and New in Tension. A look at 1 Samuel 8 should convince modern readers that religious and liturgical change and its resultant confusions are not unique to our time but an ongoing phenomenon in our tradition. Then as now, such change is most often triggered by the so-called secular.

Political movements in the ancient Near East— notably pressure from the Philistines—contributed to the establishment of the monarchy in Israel. Up until this time, Israel's faith in Yahweh had been professed simply: Yahweh was the one who promised land, who led Israel out of Egypt and through the desert. In solemn encounter he and Israel had entered into a covenant union. This Yahweh was Israel's Lord. He dwelt in a tent, was worshiped at several cultic shrines, and fought Israel's holy wars with minimal human input.

The initiation of the monarchy meant many innovations which changed Israel's political and worship life: the process of becoming a state, the establishment of the dynasty of the house of David the warrior king, and the moving of Yahweh into the Temple in Jerusalem, the political capitol. This also meant new doctrinal development which stood in tension with the old—the traditional—for centuries. A profound witness to this unresolved tension is 1 Samuel.

Israel was never of one mind on the subject of the monarchy. Some believed it of divine origin; others found it unbearable. Many believed that in David—with full possession of the land—the covenant with Abraham was fulfilled. Others saw in this new order a slighting of the Sinai covenant and its demands.

The Lord's promises to David are outlined in 2 Samuel 7:8-17: greatness for David, rest for Israel from its enemies, a Davidic heir—a son to the Lord—on the royal throne which would be firm forever. Psalm 89:4,5 sings of these promises as a covenant: "I have made a covenant with my chosen one . . . . Forever will I confirm your posterity and establish your throne for all generations." Psalm 132:12, however, while reiterating this promise of succession, includes the Davidic covenant within "my covenant" of Sinai:

"If your sons keep my covenant
    and the decrees which I shall teach them,
Their sons, too, forever
    shall sit upon your throne."

Throughout this whole process in which the new was being weighed against the old, an important pattern was emerging: Each dramatic crisis in Israel's history was accompanied and/or followed by intense theological reflection. Faced with developments (like the monarchy) in apparent contradiction to older beliefs, Israel discovered Yahweh revealing his will in the new. Thus this people was able to continue living in a viable relationship with its Lord in an ever-changing world.

And it is well that Israel could do this. The political face of the world changed so rapidly over the next few centuries and the fortunes of this people were often so adverse as to challenge the credibility of the Lord himself.

The Kingdom: Rise and Fall. David, Israel's second king, consolidated the land, bringing Israel in the north and Judah in the south under one kingship. He forced Israel's enemies to pay tribute, extended the boundaries to encompass an empire, established extensive trade and brought the nation to its zenith.

The reign of Solomon, David's son, was a time of peace, of growth in wealth and prosperity, of extensive foreign trade and much building. Solomon's greatest building project was the Temple on Mount Zion. Here, indeed, Yahweh came to dwell in the midst of his people with the king, as son, at his right hand.

Unfortunately, the Israelites misread the symbolism of Yahweh's presence. Lulled into a false sense of security by the prosperity of the new kingdom under David and Solomon, they assumed that salvation was, therefore, guaranteed; that fidelity to cultic practices was all that was required of them.

Prophets arose, anointed by Yahweh, to challenge this false sense of security. They pointed to the evils in the nation's life that set Israel on a disaster course: trust in foreign alliances rather than in Yahweh, internal social evils, cultic abuses, unworthy lives. Morally, Israel was a shambles. Within two generations after the glory of David, Judah and Israel reverted to separate kingships and an irreversible decline set in.

In less than three centuries, the northern sector (Israel) passed out of history. Conquered by the

Assyrians in 721 B.C., its citizens were deported and the land recolonized with foreigners.

Babylonia brought Judah to its final hour in 587 B.C., devastated the Temple, leveled the walls of Jerusalem, despoiled the countryside, and carried off its priests, nobles and learned men into captivity.

A half century later the rise of Persia as a world power brought release for those exiles from Judah who were willing to return to the "promised land" and endure the hardships involved in building anew. For these faith-filled people, sustained now by a new generation of prophets of hope, Cyrus the Persian King was truly "the anointed of Yahweh" who willed to recreate his people.

Judaism: World Religion

Only a small section of the original land—Jerusalem and its environs—was now available to the returning exiles. And even that was dominated politically by a foreign power. But it was enough! Officially known as the Persian province of Judah, here dwelt the remnant of Israel which the Lord had preserved for his own purposes. The most common name by which members of this remnant would henceforth be known was *Jews,* a word derived from Judah.

Beyond the geographical boundaries of the reset-tled Judah there remained, by choice or circum-stances, thousands of Jews in dispersion. For these, the essential bond of union lay neither in high politi-cal hopes nor in the promised land itself. Rather, it lay in the God of Israel, who promised better things and who challenged each generation to come to grips with his will in its own time/space situation. After a thousand years of preparation, a world religion—Judaism—was nearing the point of emergence.

Study Guide for Chapter 4

Filling In Old Testament Salvation Events

1) Read Genesis 37, part of the story of Joseph, the Jacob-descendant who went down to Egypt. Read Genesis 50:24. How does the author provide a new link with the promised land?

2) Read Exodus 1:1-4. How does the author stress the helplessness of the Hebrews? Note the concrete description.

3) Read Exodus 2:23—4:17, the earth-shattering dialogue between the Lord and Moses. Note 2:25 and 3:7—God *sees;* God *hears;* God *knows.* The Hebrew *know* means to penetrate, to share, to experience, to feel. What does this say about Israel's God?

4) Read Psalm 105:23-38 which sums up Israel's stay in Egypt and recites Yahweh's saving deeds. In the light of the prevailing belief of the ancients in nature gods, suggest why the author

shows Yahweh in power over nature.

5) Read Exodus 19 and 20. Can you visualize the setting as a dramatic liturgy of the Word? Can you see any resemblances to the liturgy of the Eucharist in Exodus 24?

6) Having entered Canaan, Joshua gathered the Israelites at Shechem—a local shrine—for a renewal of the covenant. Read Joshua 24:14-28. What do you consider the most urgent message of these verses? What section could be considered a *creed* or faith statement?

7) Read 1 Samuel 8:1-22. Note the doctrinal tension over the right of Yahweh's people to a king. Read 1 Samuel 9:14—10:1 inclusive. Note that Saul becomes the anointed commander of the Lord's people, hence, the first king.

8) God entered into a new covenant with King David. Read 2 Samuel 7:12-16 and/or Psalm 89:20-38. Refer back to the Sinai covenant, Exodus 24:3. Note the following difference: from Sinai, demands—a worthy life; from the Davidic covenant, no demands—only a promise: your kingdom shall endure forever. Could this apparent lack of demands lead to abuses?

9) Read 1 Kings 8:54-61, the address of King Solomon to Israel during the dedication of the Temple. Is Solomon aware of the Lord's ancient demands on his people? Which is the strongest of Solomon's pleas? What may he already fear?

Then Noah built an altar to the LORD, and ... he offered holocausts on the altar. When the LORD smelled the sweet odor, he said to himself, "Never again will I doom the earth because of man ...; nor will I ever again strike down all living beings, as I have done."

Genesis 8:20-21

Chapter 5

Genesis 1-11 and Its Questions

Contemporary man diligently applies himself to the task of ferreting out the story of beginnings: the origin of the universe, of planet earth, of life, of his own species. Biblical man was likewise concerned about *beginnings.* But when he compiled his primeval history, he did not possess the fine scientific tools that aid contemporary man in his search.

Of course, the motive of biblical authors was not, at base, scientific. Rather, they wished to make a faith statement—for their own people and their posterity. Therefore, Israel's story of beginnings (Genesis 1—11) emphasizes these *theological* truths:

1) Yahweh, the God who saved and created Israel, is the God who was there *in the beginning,* ordering, creating, moving.

2) Man was entrusted by God with cultural tasks. He was to dominate rather than be dominated by other creatures.

3) Man incurred sin by disobedience to God. Sin spread until it involved all mankind.

4) All men belong to God. By his command, "Be fruitful," Yahweh brought forth the nations from one stock.

At the beginning of their history (at Sinai) it would have been impossible for the Israelites to make such a faith statement about creation. The earliest Israelites had known Yahweh only as the God who made a covenant with them. Only much later—long after the formation of those early creedal references to the patriarchal promises—could other Israelites draw a direct line backwards in time from the *ongoing* creating/saving activity of God on their behalf to the creating/saving activity of God *in the beginning.*

Biblical authors were not the first of the ancients to produce a narrative descriptive of origins and the enigmatic human situation. The people of the Mesopotamian area had already authored several well-developed epics, the best known being "Enuma Elish" and "The Epic of Gilgamesh."

But one thing is sure. Though Israel's thinkers were acquainted with the form and content of this literature, they were dissatisfied with its message. While Genesis 1—11 incorporates motifs and mythological symbols from this ancient literature, the theological messages of these chapters stand in direct contradiction to it.

For example, in the Atrahasic epic, where a fragment of an old Babylonian story of the flood is preserved, the motive given for the deluge is the clamor raised by mankind. The gods cannot get their rest. Therefore, according to a quite irrational decision, mankind must be wiped out. Not so, runs the Hebrew version of the deluge (Gn 6:5ff). The one God decrees the deluge because "man's wickedness on earth" was great. With Noah he will establish a covenant and provide mankind with a fresh beginning.

Genesis and Science

Genesis 1—11 raises perennial problems for Christians struggling to relate the Bible to a contemporary worldview where science has its own story to tell about the beginnings of the universe and of man. These problems can be put in perspective by keeping the following points in mind when reading, studying or reflecting on these chapters:

1) Genesis 1—11 stands beyond the realm of empirical data. There were no eyewitnesses, no cameras, no tape recorders around when God said, "Let there be light . . . ."

2) The theology of the chapters is presented in concrete stories rather than in abstract statements.

3) As vehicles of truth, these Genesis stories must be searched for their meaning. They *picture* reality but they cannot be taken as literal accounts of actual events.

Take, for example, the first creation account (Gn 1:1—2:4a). This creation story may conflict with our contemporary scientific worldview, but it took the "science" of its own day for granted. The biblical author was comfortable making his theological points within the prevailing worldview. He made no pretense of offering any new scientific data.

The "scientific" view of the cosmos that provides the backdrop for Genesis 1 is called the three-decker universe:

Level one:	the heavens, the realm of the gods;
Level two:	the earth, the habitation of man and beast;
Level three:	the regions below—the nether world or sheol—the dwelling of the dead.

In the Genesis scenario, divine light dissipates the darkness of abysmal chaos. A dome—the sky—separates the waters above from the waters below; the waters below are collected into a single basin and allow the emergence of dry land; plant life appears. Next the heavenly luminaries establish the order of time—day and night, morning and evening. Animal life populates the waters, the sky and the dry land. Finally, man—the noblest form of life—is created and entrusted with the cultural task of ordering the earth and its creatures.

In contrast to this ordered Genesis account is the Mesopotamian "Enuma Elish." Here, working out of the same presuppositions of a three-decker universe, a very different theology unfolds. Instead of order and divine control, creation is marked by turmoil and the chaotic struggle of the gods. The creative deity Marduk, after slaying the female goddess Tiamut (the dragon of chaos), carves up the carcass and uses the material to fashion the visible universe.

Does Genesis Contradict Itself?

On the surface, apparent contradictions confront the reader of Genesis 1—11, as well as other parts of the Bible. For example, Genesis tells two different stories about creation. But some knowledge of how the sacred book was formed should be sufficient to lay the word *contradiction* to rest. *Independent traditions* are the words more frequently used by scholars to describe the various Bible stories or fragments of stories based on the same event.

The Old Testament is a composite of many books. In turn, practically every individual book represents a composite of traditions from several geographical areas or groups of peoples within Israel. And each of these traditions springs out of a variety of sources old and new.

When the Jewish editors were pulling together the literature of their people, they had one dominant purpose—to draw out the meaning of Israel's history. When the final editing of the Pentateuch (Torah)—of which Genesis 1—11 are the first chapters—was done by a group of priestly editors around 400 B.C., many decisions were made about what to include and exclude.

Sometimes two separate accounts of one event may stand side by side. Such is the case of the two stories of creation: the Priestly account (Gn 1:1—2:4a) and the Yahwist account (Gn 2:4b—3:1). These two accounts, both from southern traditions, represent the diversity which characterizes the Old Testament.

The sequence in which the priestly editor has ordered the two creation stories is a planned one. First comes the Priestly account which deals with the creation of the world and mankind *in general.* Majestic in form and lofty in thought, it reflects centuries of use in the liturgy—Israel had long celebrated her belief that God had busied himself preparing a fitting home for mankind. Second comes the Yahwist, specifically focused on man, concrete in its language and anthropomorphic in its imagery of God.

Expertly dovetailed by the editor, the two stories serve as a prelude to the story of the fall and man's growing estrangement from God—all of which set the stage for the telling of the Abraham/Isaac/Jacob narratives and the saving event of the Exodus.

Another way biblical authors dealt with diverse materials was to weave together into one account segments of various traditions with no great concern to iron out the differences. The biblical story of the Great Flood is an example of this editorial approach. Compare the Yahwist (Gn 7:2-5, 7-9) with the Priestly (Gn 6:19-20; 7—13-16). It does not bother the editor at all that the Lord in the Yahwist account specifies seven pairs of clean animals and birds and one pair of unclean animals and birds to be taken into the ark while the Priestly author limits himself to the more general "pairs of all creatures . . . male and female." The Yahwist section uses the occasion to project into the past a feature of Israel's religion: the distinction between clean and unclean animals. The Priestly section does not take this liberty.

Another example of what might be considered a conflict in the Old Testament is the story of the conquest of Canaan: one account appears in Joshua, the other in Judges 1:1—2:5. In both instances the reader must look to the meaning: the Lord led all of Israel into the Promised Land and thereby gained glory and honor.

A further example of diversity is found in the two narratives which lead up to the giving of the tables of stone on Sinai: Exodus 31 and 34 respectively. Quite neatly the editor allows for both accounts by having Moses break the original tablets (Ex 32:15-19).

The Seven Days of Creation

The seven-day model was adopted by the Priestly author from the Sumerians, an ancient Babylonian people. It offered a ready-made format for ordering the creation story. Beyond this, the author could also have intended to teach any or all of the following:

1) The week—a sacred unit of time to the Hebrews—was an original work of creation. Therefore, divine sanction was provided for man's work schedule as well as for his Sabbath rest and Sabbath worship.

2) There is a relationship between what God and man do: Both work; both rest. A divine blessing is upon the two forms of activity.

3) The Sabbath was a *sacred* day for Israel even though, for some ancients, the seventh day was a day of taboo when meaningful tasks were put aside out of fear of baneful influence.

4) Though Israel (while in exile) might be deprived of offering sacrifices, she could still—by her strict observance of Sabbath rest—confess to the importance of such cultic observances.

5) The work of creation proceeded in a serene and orderly manner under the absolute dominion of God. It was not a battle by God to gain victory over the monster of chaos as the pagan myths would have it.

The Creation of Eve

The second story of creation begins thus: "At the time when the LORD God made the earth and the heavens . . . the LORD God formed man . . . " (Gn 2:4b, 7). The Lord God then proceeds to situate the man comfortably in a garden and to provide him with a "suitable partner." When neither the birds nor the wild animals relieve the man's aloneness, the Lord God takes a rib from the man and builds it up into a woman.

The Lord God had "formed man out of the clay of the ground" (Gn 2:7). He now forms the woman out of the man—from the *'ish* (Hebrew: man) is made the *'ishah* (woman). What had before been dust and the breath of the Lord God has now by divine choice become woman.

Genesis 2:21-24 intends the *rib* to be understood symbolically. "This one shall be called 'woman,' for out of 'her man' she was taken," Adam exclaims. Thus the author reacts against the prevalent pagan view of woman: that she was of an inferior nature to man and destined to serve him. The biblical author insists that woman is equal to man, recognized as his complete counterpart. Indeed, woman *is* man; between the two there is community.

Likewise, the symbol of the rib helps the author speak to the urgent longing of the sexes for one another. This longing, implanted in man by the Creator, is satisfied when a man and woman come together in *one flesh* in a child. Thus God, right from the beginning, gives the love relationship between man and woman the dignity of the greatest creation mystery.

The Fall

Israel's polytheistic neighbors believed that dual powers of good and evil existed in the world. Each force was connected with its respective gods. Life and its tragedies reflected the interplay of these forces of good and evil—neither of which was strong enough to hold total sway.

Early Israel was not entirely free of such polytheistic notions, but continuing revelation gradually brought Israel to the point of acknowledging but one God, Yahweh. Yahweh was good and all his acts were good. Yet the perplexing fact remained: Man did live in a dual situation of good and evil. What accounted for the evil if Yahweh was truly good?

Israel concluded that evil was the doing of man. It resulted from his disobedience to Yahweh's will—which was always for the good. This reflection formed the basis for Israel's theology of the origin of sin and evil. Since memory could not carry back to the historical moment of man's original failure to measure up to the mark set for him by God, Israel set the event in *pre*-history along with the origins of the universe and man.

Israel's insight took shape in the concrete story of the fall. This story shows obvious signs of "borrowing" from other ancient literature. For example, the notion of a single pair living in perfect bliss is similar to that of Ut-napishtim and his wife, survivors of the flood, in "The Epic of Gilgamesh." The tree of life is common in Mesopotamian literature and art. The image of the cherubim stationed "to guard the way to the tree of life" (Gn 3:24) is drawn from Babylonian mythology to express Hebrew belief in heavenly messengers. The flaming sword is another mythological image, probably meant here as lightning flashes symbolic of Yahweh's anger. All these elements assist the narrator of Israel's story in witnessing to the unique personal testimony of his people.

The story draws an accurate picture of the psychological process in which any and every sinner has been engaged: attraction, temptation, consent, sin, shame, fear—even the transferral of guilt from self to another.

And sin was not experienced by Israel as merely private or personal in its effects. Therefore, this "original sin" is linked in a causal way with certain fundamental disorders in the human condition: the ongoing struggle with evil; the sweat and toil of human existence; woman's dependance on man, and the pangs she endures in fulfilling her creative role; even death.

Cain and Abel

When the biblical authors set themselves to teaching about the spread of evil, they did so in the context of stories already in existence. These anecdotes, culled from folklore, legend and pagan mythology had been created in response to such questions as "Why the great flood?" and "Why different languages?" Reworked and brought in line with Israel's faith, they were linked together by the use of genealogies (Gn 5) and the Table of the Nations (Gn 10) to form a continuing testimony to man's sinfulness and its far-reaching impact.

One such anecdote, presumably with a Mesopotamian background, dealt with the ongoing feud between herdsman and farmer. The finished biblical version traces the root of the problem back to the original fall and makes the characters, Cain and Abel, the sons of Adam and Eve. The story in its present form reflects the conflict between nomadic Israelites and the settled Canaanites early in the conquest of the promised land. Cain is like the Canaanite farmers; Abel is like the Israelite herdsmen. Five million years ago when man put in his appearance on the earth, there were neither herds nor cultivated gardens!

In this concise narrative (Gn 4), the Hebrew author: 1) begins the story of man's gradual moral deterioration which culminates in the flood and a new beginning for man; 2) depicts Abel as a pastoral culture hero, the first herdsman; 3) lauds the superiority of the sacrifice of the nomad over that of the peasant.

The Question of Longevity

The biblical author didn't know how long man's early ancestors lived. And science now points to an even shorter life span for man 3,000 and more years ago than today. Yet the Genesis stories speak of men living for hundreds of years.

Most of the long-lived persons of Genesis 5 are mentioned in connection with genealogies. These could have been constructed in conscious imitation of such listings belonging to other peoples. One record of Babylonian kings testifies to several reigns of more than 100,000 years!

The assignment of longevity also has symbolic import. It was the author's way of saying that a particular man was very wise and good. Therefore, to certain persons *many years* were attributed, to other persons *fewer years.*

The decline in longevity was also a graphic way to describe the effects of evil. As sin mounted in the world, mankind in general was less good and less wise; therefore, man's years were fewer.

Noah and the Deluge

Several cultures had long preserved the memory of a particularly disastrous and far-reaching flood in the area of the Tigris and Euphrates Rivers. These non-Israelite accounts of the catastrophe attribute the flood to a capricious act of the gods.

To date, three extra-biblical stories have been discovered. One describes the deluge as a divine scheme to destroy men because they disturbed the rest of the gods. The hero is warned of the deluge by a sympathetic god who instructs him to build a large boat, bring provisions, and take craftsmen with him so that human arts do not perish.

The resemblances between such an account and that of Genesis are numerous. But instead of attributing the flood to the irrational anger of the gods, the biblical story lays the blame on *man's* wickedness. Here we have another example of the common Hebrew practice of adapting an already existing story to make their own point.

The biblical author adds on to the narrative of the flood a series of *first things;* that is, the answers to certain human concerns and questions:

1) In response to Noah's sacrifice, the Lord pledged the stability of the seasons (Gn 8:22).

2) The use of flesh meat was now justified by divine permission. "Only flesh with its life-blood still in it you shall not eat" (Gn 9:3-5).

3) The rainbow originated as a sign of God's covenant with man and beast (Gn 9:8-17).

4) Noah is a culture hero; he originated vine culture. "Now Noah, a man of the soil, was the first to plant a vineyard" (Gn 9:20).

5) The enslavement of the Canaanites by the Israelites is justified by Noah: "Cursed be Canaan (the son of Ham): The lowest of slaves shall he be to his brother" (Gn 9:18-27).

6) After the flood other nations of the earth are seen as branching out from the sons of Noah: Shem, Ham and Japhet (Gn 10).

Tower of Babel

With the original sin the first man alienated himself from his God and his fellowmen. In the story of the Tower of Babel, we see the culmination of sin and its effects—all human society is depicted as alienated from its God and from one another. Sinfulness is defined in the story as the human desire to *make a name* for ourselves through cultural achievement rather than through a proper relationship to God.

To make this theological point, the biblical author has borrowed an ancient Mesopotamian story which proposed to tell of the origin of languages. The tower, a titanic undertaking, was a Babylonian ziggurat built in stages or levels. The Hebrew adaptation of the story is reflected in the poor quality building materials used: the stone and mortar common to Palestine.

For mankind *in general,* this is the end of the road. Up till this point, a particular story of sin ends with a benevolent act of God: God clothes Adam and Eve and permits them to live; God puts a saving mark on Cain; God follows the flood with a new beginning. But here the story ends without grace: All nations are in a state of alienation from God.

Only in Genesis 12:1-3 do we see that God will continue to act in man's behalf with a plan for the salvation of the nations:

> The LORD said to Abram: "Go forth from the land of your kinsfolk and from your father's house to a land that I will show you.
>
> "I will make of you a great nation,
> and I will bless you;
> I will make your name great,
> so that you will be a blessing....
> All the communities of the earth
> shall find blessing in you."

Thus the first 11 chapters of Genesis set the stage for the telling of Israel's *history* and her experience of a God who reveals himself and acts through that *history.* In these chapters of prehistory, Israel looks back beyond her own history to relate her experience of a creating/saving God and the human condition with the story of beginnings and the origin of the human condition.

Study Guide for Chapter 5

Looking Further Into Genesis 1-11

1) "In the beginning God created ...." God brought order out of chaos. Read Genesis 1, the Priestly story of creation. How many times does the word *good* appear? What point is the author making?

2) The religion of other ancient people was often a nature religion: sun, moon, stars, waters were connected with the gods. How does the Priestly author of Genesis 1 show this is not the case with the Israelites?

3) God said to the man and to the woman, "Be fruitful, fill the earth and subdue it." Scan Genesis 5, the genealogy of the descendants of Adam and Eve. From one stock the nations stem. Note, too, the direct historical line from Adam, the disobedient man, to Noah, the obedient man in whom mankind has a new beginning (see Gn 6:22).

4) Read Genesis 3:4 where the serpent lies to the woman and denies the real punishment of sin. Read Genesis 3:16-19. This is the penalty of sin as Israel views it.

5) The "tree of life" was a common ancient symbol of immortality (Gn 2:9). Read Genesis 3:19; then, 3:22-24. Note the connection between the two references: Death is the lot of sinful man.

6) Read Genesis 2:23; then, 3:20. Man's wife is first called *woman,* then *Eve.* Sin has brought death but life will continue. Can you grasp the author's skill as he gives meaning to the name of the woman?

7) The Yahwist tradition often speaks of God in an anthropomorphic manner—that is, it gives God human characteristics or manners. Read the following: Genesis 2:7; 2:19; 2:21,22; 3:21; 6:6; 6:7; 7:16b; 8:21. What is the anthropomorphism in each?

8) From observation primitive man knew that the seasons were stable. Read Genesis 8:22. Note

how the ancients recognized the hand of God even in apparently ordinary events. Suggest why we are prone to split our world into two parts: the sacred and the secular. Would you consider this practice a value or a disvalue on our part?

9) Read Genesis 3:22-24—man's alienation from God. Read Genesis 4:1-16—man's alienation from his fellowmen. Read Genesis 11:1-9—the alienation of all human society from God and men from one another. Discuss sin from the viewpoint of alienation in your own life and contemporary society.

10) With Abraham's appearance Genesis takes on a new tone. Read Genesis 11:26—12:3. Note how God "sorts" Abraham out from the descendants of one of Noah's sons, Shem. Whereas man had been turning *from* God, now man begins turning *toward* God.

On the day the LORD spoke to Moses in Egypt he said, ... "See I have made you as God to Pharaoh, and Aaron your brother shall act as your prophet. ..." Moses was eighty years old and Aaron eighty-three when they spoke to Pharaoh.

Exodus 6:28; 7:1,6,7

Chapter 6

The Prophet: Man Appointed by Yahweh

Seek good and not evil
   that you may live;
Then truly will the LORD, the God of hosts,
   be with you as you claim!
Hate evil and love good,
   and let justice prevail at the gate.
Then it will be that the LORD, the God of
      hosts,
   will have pity on the remnant of Joseph.

(Am 5:14-15)

Thus Amos the prophet spoke to the people of Israel in his day, eight centuries before the birth of Jesus. Thus might the prophet *still* speak to the people of God in our day, nearly 20 centuries after the birth of Jesus. There is a certain universality to the message of the biblical prophet.

Who Is the Prophet?

Who were these men who rose out of obscurity to become a national institution in Israel?

Our English word *prophet* is derived from the Greek *prophetes,* meaning one who speaks before others. *Prophetes,* in turn, is a translation of the Hebrew *nabi: one called* (by God to speak for him).

Ancient manuscripts give reason to assume that prophecy was introduced to Israel from the surrounding cultures of Mesopotamia. Israel, however, transformed the institution of prophecy in a way unparalleled by other people in the area. Hebrew prophecy is unique in its ethical and religious content.

As used in the Old Testament the word *prophet* is a broad term. It refers to the classical—or writing—prophets, the men we are more apt to think of when someone mentions the words "biblical prophet." For example, men like Jeremiah, Amos and Isaiah. But *prophet* also refers to certain other persons who played a distinctive role in Israel's history and these likewise deserve notice.

Though Moses is considered a prophet and traces of prophetic activity are found in his time, it was not until the period of the late Judges and early monarchy that prophecy became a recognized institution in Israel. Two types appear: ecstatic groups of prophets and individual prophets like Samuel.

The bands of prophets lived a common life in which they developed their spirituality. They were generally associated with a particular site from which they went forth to teach the people and encourage fidelity to Yahweh, the God of the covenant. Distinguished in garb by their hair mantles, they reached the ecstatic state through a combination of frenetic movement or dance and music. In this state they prophesied. A band of such prophets met Saul as he was on his way to Gibeah, a site to which they were attached (1 Sam 10:5-13).

Elijah and Elisha, though they acted as individual prophets, were both leaders of groups of prophets in northern Israel in the ninth century. These communities were associated with cultic sites located at Bethel, Jericho and Gilgal (2 Kgs 2:1ff; 4:38ff; 9:1ff).

Samuel—called both "seer" and prophet—was a close associate of the ecstatic prophets (1 Sm 19:20) and was an advisor of the king in spiritual matters (1 Sm 13:8-15). Samuel preached that the word of God was the important factor in Israel's history and that obedience was preferable to sacrifice. This emphasis of the great prophet gave direction to prophetism for centuries.

It was not uncommon for the prophetic spirit to be centered in individuals who were involved with the political situation of the nation. These men, loyal to Yahweh and undaunted by persecution, thought it well within their role to instruct kings concerning national policies, to reprove them on occasion for failures in personal morality and to predict events. Nathan, who served in David's court, was such a prophet (2 Sm 7:1-17); likewise was Ahijah, a prophet from Shiloh, an advisor to King Jeroboam I (1 Kgs 14:1-21); and also Elijah and Elisha.

There were even whole bands of prophets closely

tied to the political situation. One such group was stationed next to a Philistine garrison (1 Sm 10:5-7). Intensely patriotic, their aim was to incite Israelites to engage in a holy war against the enemy. (See also 1 Kgs 27.)

In a word, these early non-classical prophets, with the exception of a few time-servers—false prophets—were loyal Yahwists who considered Israel's traditions, laws and customs as norms not to be easily set aside.

Appearing at the height of the prophetic impulse in Israel are the *classical,* or writing, prophets. Their message was so powerful that it has effectively influenced the history of the western hemisphere—if not of the world.

The writing prophets have been divided into two groups—the *major prophets* and the *minor prophets*—solely on the length of their books. Due to the nature of their message the earlier classical prophets are sometimes called *prophets of doom* and later prophets, for example, Ezekiel, are often titled *prophets of hope.*

The Lot of the Prophet. Serving the Lord as prophet did not guarantee one any esteemed position in either Israel or Judah. Abuse, expulsion and imprisonment were commonly the lot of men like Amos and Jeremiah who spoke out against the moral turpitude of a covenant people and prophesied punishment and death, dissolution and/or captivity. No wonder kings and princes, priests and (*false*) prophets sought to stay their tongue. The word of the Lord must be contained!

Whether or not the authorities succeeded in containing the word is another question altogether. Jeremiah tells us that when, due to persecution, he tried not to speak it became "like fire burning in my heart, imprisoned in my bones" (Jer 20:9b). Even when the message of the Lord fell on closed hearts, the classical prophets circumvented that closedness by committing their message to writing. Later generations pondered and learned from the message which these chosen ones had preached.

The Decline of Prophecy. After the return from the Babylonian exile, prophecy went into a gradual decline. Later prophets lacked the vigor of their predecessors. And devotion to the law eventually preempted the spoken word of the prophet as the main locus of God's revelatory will. The scribe, as interpreter of the law, became the guide of Israel's faith. Meanwhile, a resurgence of prophecy was hoped for in the indefinite future.

Space does not permit a consideration of each of the classical prophets. But a limited discussion of several prophets—Amos, Hosea, Isaiah and Jeremiah—can give a feel for prophetism in Israel during a particular period of history and in a particular place.

The word of God was never uttered in a vacuum or from an ivory tower. It is of the essence of Israelite prophecy that it relates to a sense of history, of destiny, of God acting here and now in the world. In fact, some scholars relate the decline of prophecy to the fact that after the exile, with Israel no longer a power on the world stage, some of that sense of history and destiny was lost.

Amos: Sheepherder Become Prophet

King David succeeded in forming a united kingdom of Israel. Two generations later Israel again became a kingdom divided: Israel in the north; Judah in the south. Judah acknowledged Rehoboam, son of Solomon, as its king. Israel claimed Jeroboam, son of Nebat, for its ruler. It was in the northern kingdom of Israel that both Hosea and Amos prophesied.

Under Jeroboam II (786-746 B.C.) the north enjoyed a resurgence of material prosperity. At the same time moral decay was on the rise.

Onto this scene stepped Amos, a sheepherder from Tekoa, a town of Judah. He was not a prophet or a member of a company of prophets as described above. Yet Amos felt the pull of a new vocation which he was powerless to resist: "The Lord took me from following the flock, and said to me, Go, prophesy to my people Israel" (Am 7:15). And prophesy, however reluctantly, Amos did. His "arena" was the royal shrine at Bethel.

The book of Amos, as most prophetic books, is a collection of oracles—judgments, discourses and visions—compiled either personally or by disciples. Over the centuries the process of transmission and adaptation allowed certain elements of hope to find their way into the book. Thus, hope prevails in the closing verses of the book:

> I will bring about the restoration of my people
>> Israel;
>>> they shall rebuild and inhabit their ruined
>>> cities,
>> Plant vineyards and drink the wine,

set out gardens and eat the fruits.
I will plant them upon their own ground;
    never again shall they be plucked
From the land I have given them,
    says I, the LORD, your God. (Am 9:14, 15)
But for the most part, Amos deserves the label
"prophet of doom."

The *written* Amos begins by pronouncing a judgment on Israel's neighbors, including Judah. But
beginning with chapter 2:6, he turns the tables on an
unsuspecting, complacent Israel and rails against her
social crimes—oppression of the poor and the un-
natural pursuit of wealth:

Because they sell the just man for silver,
    and the poor man for a pair of sandals.
They trample the heads of the weak
    into the dust of the earth,
    and force the lowly out of the way....
For they know not how to do what is right,
    says the LORD,
Storing up in their castles
    what they have extorted and robbed.
               (Am 2:6, 7; 3:10)

A covenant people was failing its covenant Lord.
Such lack of zeal for justice on the home front was
destined to be reflected in sheer weakness on the international front: "An enemy shall surround the
land, and strip you of your strength, and pillage your
castles" (Am 3:11).

Israel's leaders felt the nation had a unilateral
guarantee of divine benediction. This conviction
was, doubtlessly, based on the *unconditional* nature
of the covenant promise made to David (see 2 Sm
7:8ff). But the role of the prophet was to disillusion

these leaders. The Sinai covenant—and its *obligations*—had not been superseded! There was nothing magical about Yahweh's way of salvation.

The proliferation of sacrifices and tithes and publicly proclaimed freewill offerings would not satisfy Yahweh. The reason? These symbolic gifts were empty when their donors were living selfish lives. Justice and righteousness are what counts. Worship of God—yes, but not a cult grown dangerously superstitious:

> I hate, I spurn your feasts,
>> I take no pleasure in your solemnities....
> Away with your noisy songs!...
> But if you would offer me holocausts,
>> then let justice surge like water,
>> and goodness like an unfailing stream.

(Am 5:21,23)

Despite Yahweh's invitations to his people to repent, the prophet knew that the end was already in sight. Amos pronounced the word that kings would prefer went unspoken:

> The eyes of the Lord GOD are on this sinful
>> kingdom:
> I will destroy it from the face of the earth.

(Am 9:8)

Hosea: Prophet of Unrequited Love

Since Hosea likewise prophesied during the reign of Jeroboam II, he was either a contemporary or near-contemporary of Amos. Unlike Amos, he was a native of Israel.

Hosea began the tradition of describing the relationship between the nation and its God in terms of marriage imagery. Within this framework he worked out his message to the people.

Hosea's prophetic vocation seems to have been precipitated by a personal domestic tragedy. Gomer, his wife, proved unfaithful—maybe even participating in the sacred prostitution peculiar to the worship of the pagan deities. This painful experience of love accepted and later rejected was suggestive to Hosea of what had come to pass between Yahweh and Israel.

The book of Hosea does not make for easy reading. It contains both biographical and autobiographical material and is often fragmentary. At places the distinction between Gomer and Israel is blurred.

But the prophet's overall message breaks into bold relief: Israel is the espoused of Yahweh. She has played the harlot. In all justice, despite moments of intense compassion, Yahweh has no alternative but to permit the historical Israel to perish. Only in a new beginning in the desert is there hope.

The manner of Israel's harlotry is not made clear by the prophet. Israel may have been worshiping Baal—the fertility god. Or she may have been worshiping Yahweh as a fertility deity. No doubt both irregularities occurred.

For Hosea there was but one God: Yahweh. The prosperity and safety of the nation, the fertility of land and beast were all dependent on Israel's fidelity to Yahweh alone:

> Since she has not known
> > that it was I who gave her
> > the grain, the wine, and the oil....
> Therefore I will take back my grain in its time

and my wine in its season;
I will snatch away my wool and my flax....
I will lay waste her vines and fig trees....

(Hos 2:10-14)

Social evils, too, troubled the prophet:

... for the LORD has a grievance
against the inhabitants of the land:
There is no fidelity, no mercy,
no knowledge of God in the land.
False swearing, lying, murder, stealing and
adultery!
in their lawlessness, bloodshed follows
bloodshed. (Hos 4:1,2)

Even the *land* is under affliction because of the perfidy of its inhabitants.

Therefore, the land mourns,
and everything that dwells in it languishes.

(Hos 4:3)

Hosea is an artisan with words; a master of his people's history; a devotee of tradition; an Israelite committed to the Sinai covenant. He is a shrewd observer of human behavior; a harsh critic of human infidelity. He is a lover of Yahweh; a man given to intense levels of anger and tenderness.

His words have an inexhaustible power and depth of meaning. Yet there is a forthrightness and simplicity in Hosea's statement of Yahweh's yearnings: "It is love that I desire, not sacrifice, and knowledge of God rather than holocausts" (Hos 6:6).

A love response, an openness to penetration by the lover—this was the will of God for his people. Only within such a renewed dialogue could come the healing which divine love is capable of generating:

"I will heal their defection, I will love them freely" (Hos 14:5).

But Israel did not hear. With the covenant forgotten, with internal decay both expressed in and aggravated by political intrigue, Israel found herself incapable of dealing with the Assyrians who coveted her lands. By 722/721 B.C. the Assyrians had come, had conquered and had established themselves as rulers. The northern kingdom of Israel was destroyed, never again to arise. Thousands of its citizens were deported and vanished from history.

Isaiah: Prophet Who Gives Balance

Meanwhile, Judah was not free of the disease that had brought ruin upon Israel. The difference was but one of degree.

Though reforms were eventually initiated to insure fulfillment of the demands of the Mosaic covenant, a bogus sense of security prevailed. Come what may, the prevailing attitude said, our Temple, the Davidic kingship and our state are guaranteed perpetuity under the Davidic covenant.

Isaiah of Jerusalem. A towering personality, he was Yahweh's prophet to Judah for roughly 50 years. Beginning with his call in 742 B.C., he served during a time of impending national tragedy spearheaded by Assyrian aggressiveness and compounded by the dangerous smugness already outlined. The book of Isaiah, for reasons given below, can be divided into three main sections. Only the first 39 chapters contain material which can be connected with Isaiah of Jerusalem.

Isaiah's denunciations of Judah were fully within the doom and gloom tradition of Amos. Yet Isaiah treasured the ideal of the perpetuation of the Davidic kingship and of Jerusalem (Zion) as the center of salvation. Thus, Yahweh's plan to establish his kingly rule for peace would not be thwarted; hope need not be surrendered. In the present tragedy the wicked would be purged and a purified, chastened remnant would be left (see Is 25:5ff; 37:30-32).

Second Isaiah. In the book of Isaiah we meet a phenomenon common in ancient literature: the custom of attaching certain traditions or stories to a famous person for the purpose of attracting attention to them. Thus, much of Israel's wisdom literature is attributed to Solomon, the nation's third king. And Moses is credited as Israel's lawgiver though many of the laws gathered up in the Moses tradition belong to a much later period. Thus it is with Isaiah and the book which bears his name. This famous prophet never saw the latter chapters of the book of Isaiah or the period of Israel's history which they reflect.

Chapters 40-55 are credited to an anonymous person whom scholars call Second Isaiah. Three reasons are given for suggesting a different author for this section:

1) *Historical.* The words are addressed to the deported Judeans in Babylon between 550 B.C. and 540 B.C. Cyrus, a threat to Babylon and the liberator of Israel, was on the throne of Persia (Is 41:1-5).

2) *Doctrinal.* Monotheism is more highly developed than in Isaiah's day where other gods

might exist, but Yahweh was Israel's God and certainly the mightiest and most powerful of gods: "I am the first and I am the last; there is no God but me" (Is 44:6). Likewise, the notion of deliverance by a Messiah (an anointed one) is developed beyond that of the early chapters (Is 44:28—45:1).

3) *Literary.* Unlike the early chapters there is a highly emotional tone to the writing, and the language is rich and hymnic in nature. Second Isaiah is so sanguine about the imminent delivery of Israel from exile in Babylon that he announces that the kingdom of God is at hand:

> Go up onto a high mountain,
>   Zion, herald of glad tidings;
> Cry out at the top of your voice...!
> Here comes with power
>   the Lord GOD,
>   who rules by his strong arm.   (Is 40:9-10)

He even sings of messianic glory:

> Raise a glad cry, you heavens:
>   the LORD has done this;
>   shout, you depths of the earth.
> Break forth, you mountains, into song,
>   You forest, with all your trees.
> For the LORD has redeemed Jacob,
>   and shows his glory through Israel.
>
>   (Is 44:23)

Second Isaiah contains the four Servant Songs (Isaiah 42:1-4; 49:1-7; 50:4-11; 52:13—53:12). According to these songs, salvation is won through the servant of the Lord.

> Here is my servant, whom I uphold,
>   my chosen one with whom I am pleased,
> Upon whom I have put my spirit;

he shall bring forth justice to the nations.

(Is 42:1)

Because the servant identifies with suffering men, he shall be considered great; special redeeming powers will be his:

Because he surrendered himself to death
and was counted among the wicked;
And he shall take away the sins of many,
and win pardon for their offenses. (Is 53:12b)

The identity of this servant who will carry out God's purpose of universal salvation has continued to vex Scripture commentators. Is the servant the people of Israel or a remnant of Israel? Is the servant a person? Perhaps even Second Isaiah himself? Though the problem must be left open to debate, the Servant Songs have been linked with the New Testament teaching about Jesus. Jesus suffered innocently in the place of others and gained pardon for their offenses.

Third Isaiah. Nearly another century later—around 450 B.C.—another collection of writings were placed in the book of Isaiah: chapters 56-66. Now the locale is Palestine, not Babylon. In this section of Isaiah there is much moral exhortation.

Those desiring the Lord's salvation must practice social justice: the release of the unjustly bound, the untying of the thongs of the yoke, the setting free of the oppressed, the breaking of every yoke:

Sharing your bread with the hungry,
sheltering the oppressed and the homeless;
Clothing the naked when you see them,
and not turning your back on your own.

(Is 58:7)

Isaiah 56:1-8 sees salvation as intended for all: the dispersed of Israel, eunuchs, foreigners. Participation in this salvation of the Lord will be grounded in observance of the covenant:

> Observe what is right, do what is just;
>> for my salvation is about to come,
>> my justice about to be revealed.
> All who keep the sabbath free from profanation
>> and hold to my covenant,
> Them I will bring to my holy mountain
>> and make joyful in my house of prayer.

> (Is 56:1,6,7)

No longer shall the sound of weeping be heard in Jerusalem. Long life and peace, enjoyment of home and product of the field belong to the blessings of the new creation (Is 65:17-25).

Thus there is a broad sweep to the book of Isaiah: It embraces nearly 300 years; it reaches from Judea to Babylonia and back to Judea; and it outlines the spiritual development of the people of God at three stages of its history: 1) Isaiah of Jerusalem indicts his people (Judah) for social injustices and inauthentic worship and warns against foreign alliances. He pronounces doom, yet grants the possibility of hope. 2) Second Isaiah (Deutero-Isaiah) in exile in Babylonia raises hope, promises salvation. 3) Third Isaiah (Trito-Isaiah), at home again in a decimated Judea struggles with apostasy and sin, preaches deliverance and pulses with hope.

This tapestry of prophetic thought woven by so many minds over so many centuries strikes a balance between the darkness of doom and destruction and the brilliance of a new creation. It stands as a permanent witness to the enduring faith of a people—

Israel—who never forgot that the Lord God is *with* them and *for* them.

Jeremiah: Prophet Who Sees New Things

Jeremiah was Yahweh's anointed one immediately prior to and during the time of the Babylonian assault upon the south. As was characteristic of the prophet, Jeremiah surveyed the situation in his day, reflected in the Spirit with which he had been anointed, and spoke. His message: Disaster is coming from the north (Babylonia) because Judah has given itself over to Baal worship:

> I will pronounce my sentence against them
>   for all their wickedness in forsaking me,
> And in burning incense to strange gods
>   and adoring their own handiwork. (Jer 1:16)

Jeremiah's famous address (Jer 7:1-15) at the gate of the Temple was a direct *word of the Lord* and a plea, "Reform your ways and your deeds." Even Temple worship offered no national security blanket: Unless reform set in, the Lord would take his departure. Judah's center of worship would be destroyed even as was Israel's shrine at Shiloh.

Whereas little is known of the personal history of the earlier prophets, the book of Jeremiah contains both biography and autobiography. This new development evidences the insight that the *man* and his *message* cannot be separated.

And indeed, we would not care to overlook this man. Jeremiah is so variously complex that each of us can identify a bit of ourself in him. Jeremiah agonizes: "You duped me, O Lord, and I let myself be duped; You were too strong for me, and you triumphed" (Jer 20:7). And he demands: "Remember me, Lord, visit me, and avenge me on my persecutors" (Jer 15:15).

Beyond the hour of darkness precipitated by Babylonian victory and the exile in 598 B.C., Jeremiah saw "a future full of hope" (Jer 29:11). In reality, the salvation of the Lord would come *by way of Babylon*. Purified, the exiles—the good figs— would return to be formed into a *new* Israel. Externally, all would be restored to normal. Internally, the needed radical change would be effected: "I will give them a heart with which to understand that I am the Lord. They shall be my people and I will be their God, for they shall return to me with all their heart" (Jer 24:7).

The book of Jeremiah offers further hope for the people of God. The Lord will make a new and everlasting covenant with them. All, "from least to greatest," will know his law without being taught: "I will...write it upon their hearts" (Jer 31:31-34).

In drawing out the fuller meaning of Jeremiah's prophecy, Christian theologians turn to Jesus. In him and through him this new covenant was enacted. Incorporation into Jesus at Baptism makes a person a member of the new covenant community.

A New Beginning

In 587 B.C. Nebuchadnezzar, King of Babylonia, arrived to settle accounts with the ever rebellious kingdom of Judah. But even before the fall of the city and the deportation to Babylonia, Yahweh raised up another prophet to his people—Ezekiel. His task was to provide the hopeful message to sustain the people in exile.

For Ezekiel the time was ripe for a newly creative act. In this event, the Lord would regenerate his people—not for their sake, but for the sake of his holy name which Israel had profaned among the nations: "Thus the nations shall know that I am the Lord....I will sprinkle clean water upon you....I will give you a new heart and place a new spirit within you...." (Ez 36:23-28)

Cyrus, King of Persia and conqueror of Babylonia in 539 B.C., was the anointed of the Lord, the one who would enable Judah to rise again and move into a new phase of history:

> He shall say of Jerusalem, "Let her be rebuilt,"
> and of the temple, "Let its foundations
> be laid." (Is 44:28b)

Prophecy in Israel and Beyond

1) In line with such admonitions as that of Amos 5:14-15, write a prophetic warning for today's world.

2) In Israel's faith, the word of the Lord once spoken was always *effective*. Read Amos 7:17— doom pronounced on Israel by the prophet. Can you see why Amaziah said to Amos, "Off with you visionary . . . [N]ever again prophesy in Bethel" (Am 7:12-13)?

3) In contrast to the great poverty of the masses, Israel's self-centered rulers loved luxury. Read Amos 6:4-6. Can a nation which ignores and/or oppresses its poor remain "healthy" for long? Explain your answer.

4) God's love for Israel is tenderly expressed by Hosea. Read Hosea 11:1-4 in which he parallels this love and Israel's ungrateful response. Yet

God cannot give up his people. Read Hosea 11:8-9. Note the very human, emotional tones of God's address.

5) History witnesses that chaos results when law and order lose control. Read Isaiah 3:13-15. What reason does Isaiah—a man of faith—give for the disorder in Judah?

6) Second Isaiah writes of a *suffering servant* who "was pierced for our offenses, crushed for our sins" (Is 53:5). Because of identity with the *servant*, Israel will rise again. Read Isaiah 53:11-12. Why do Christians identify Christ with the servant? Read Isaiah 53:4-10. How many parallels are there with the story told of the passion of Jesus?

7) Jeremiah wished for a hideaway from sinful Judah. Read Jeremiah 9:1-8. What has happened to a covenant people? Even God must do more to bring about salvation. Read Jeremiah 31:31-34; also, the footnote. See Luke 22:20 and 1 Corinthians 11:25.

8) For Ezekiel the time was ripe for a newly creative act. Read his famous "Vision of the Dry Bones" (Ez 37:1-15). Note how the ancients created a dramatic spectacle to carry a message—in this instance: Israel will rise again.

Thus the Levites keep your words,
    and your covenant they uphold.
They promulgate your decisions to Jacob
    and your law to Israel.

Deuteronomy 33:9-10

Chapter 7

Law:
The Will of Yahweh

Israel had not chosen its God; Yahweh had chosen Israel. As Moses declares: "You are a people sacred to the LORD, your God; he has chosen you from all the nations on the face of the earth to be a people peculiarly his own" (Dt 7:6). A sign of Israel's "chosenness" was the invitation to enter into a covenant union. And "the Law" was Israel's response to this covenant—her attempt to work out a worthy pattern of life within the context of this relationship.

These life patterns became increasingly regulated. Seen as flowing directly from the will of Yahweh, they were expressed in obligatory commandments, statutes and degrees: "Understand, then, that the LORD, your God, is God indeed, the faithful

God who keeps his covenant down to the thousandth generation toward those who love him and keep his commandments . . . You shall therefore carefully observe the commandments, the statutes and the decrees which I enjoin on you today" (Dt 7:9,11).

Observance of the law was a matter of life or death for Israel. Moses proclaims: "I call heaven and earth today to witness against you. I have set before you life and death . . . . Choose life, then, that you and your descendants may live, by loving the LORD your God, heeding his voice, and holding fast to him" (Dt 30:19, 20).

The following sequence in the early God-Israel relationship is all-important in understanding the origins of the law: 1) Yahweh elects Israel; 2) Yahweh invites Israel to a covenant union; 3) Yahweh gives Israel laws to guide this covenant life.

Hence law, a worthy response to the graciousness of God, followed logically upon covenant. And since the covenant agreement was initially articulated by Moses on Mt. Sinai, each of Israel's growing legal traditions would, in its turn, be attributed to Moses and Sinai.

The covenant between God and Israel was the beginning of an original history, a history which God and his people would make together. In the course of this history, the conduct of Israel would be guided by *torah* (the Hebrew word meaning law; later signified the formal collection of laws). The basis of this God-inspired conduct would be love; its fruit would be action and service. Through concrete deeds God and his covenant people would work together for salvation. A new activity was abroad in the world!

Sinai was not a closed event; it was a *living experience* opening out as each generation, in relation to Yahweh, struggled to live out its covenant response in ever-changing situations. Therefore, Israel's law continually developed as an exposition of God's revealed will for his covenant people.

Many separate strands of law date from Moses (13th century B.C.) to the Babylonian Exile. The various strands or collections found in the Pentateuch include:

1) The Ten Commandments, which will be discussed in the next section.

2) The Book of the Covenant, found in Exodus 20:22—23:33. The title is derived from Exodus 24:7, "Taking the book of the covenant, he [Moses] read it aloud to the people." After the *ten words*, this Code of the Covenant is considered the oldest of the codes. Its date is ascertained by a consideration of the social and economic background witnessed by its regulations. The period of the nomad is past; the Israelites now live in houses, own oxen and cultivate fields and vineyards. But the absence of reference to trade or commerce indicates a date earlier than the monarchy (10th century B.C.). Much of this code derives from older customary law which may have passed into Israelite hands during the period of the Judges.

The decalogue had only fenced off Israel's life in a negative form: *Thou shalt not . . . .* Now the field within that fence was given a divine order by the variety of positive commands in the Book of the Covenant. Three classes of laws are contained in it:

  a) Civil and penal laws: for example, "Whoever strikes a man a mortal blow must be put to death" (21:12).

b) Laws of worship: for example, "If you make an altar of stone for me, do not build it out of cut stone, for by putting a tool to it you desecrate it" (20:25).

c) Laws controlling morality: for example, "You shall not wrong any widow or orphan" (22:21).

The humanitarian and religious laws of this Covenant Code witness a higher level of development than found in surrounding cultures. These are probably Israelite in origin.

3) The Ritual Decalogue in Exodus 34:17-27, so-called because cultic concerns dominate. Images are prohibited and certain festivals and offerings are legislated. This Ritual Decalogue is regarded as one of Israel's oldest collections and contains some of its earliest cultic customs.

4) The Deuteronomic Code in Deuteronomy 12 to 26. Based upon the customary law of other ancient Near Eastern peoples it can be read, according to some scholars, as a code drawn up for use at a sanctuary—for example, Shechem, in the north. Other scholars view the collection as a program intended to undergird a great religious and national revival at a time when the future looked bleak due to the growing threat from Assyria. This latter notion would date the Code somewhere before 721 B.C., the date of northern Israel's demise in the face of an Assyrian invasian.

5) The Law of Holiness in Leviticus 17—26:41 was the inspiration of much of the later Priestly tradition. First compiled before 586 B.C. by the clergy in Jerusalem from earlier laws, this collection was

later broadened to include laws dating from the Babylonian exile and after. According to the Law of Holiness, the Israelite must be holy because the Lord is holy (Lev 19:2). Both legal and moral purity belong to this holiness.

6) The Priestly or Sacerdotal Code, scattered throughout the Pentateuch in the various strands of the Priestly tradition (for example: Lev 1-7, the ritual of sacrifices; Lev 11-15, laws regarding legal purity; Num 28-29, laws about food-offerings at festivals). The Priestly tradition was presumably compiled after the exile as a law for priests, but some of the cultic-ritual laws were added even later.

Originally the various collections listed above existed as separate units. But eventually the growing body of Israel's law was recognized as a single entity: the *Torah of Yahweh.* It was edited and compiled and recorded in Exodus 20 through Numbers 10:10 and in much of Deuteronomy as well. Since the books which contain this law are the first five books of the Bible, they are referred to as the Pentateuch (from the Greek, *pentateuchos,* consisting of five books). And these five books of law are also called the Torah.

The word *torah* does not refer simply to law as inscribed in a book. Rather, it emphasizes the law as *priestly instruction,* and, therefore, as God's revelation given through the priests.

The Ten Commandments

That God gave "ten words" to Moses on Mt. Sinai is deeply imbedded in the Hebrew tradition. In Exodus 24:7 we read: "Taking the book of the covenant, he read it aloud to the people, who answered, 'All that the LORD has said, we will heed and do.' " Scholars generally agree that the "book of the covenant" which Moses read was the "ten words" or, as we have come to call them, the Ten Commandments.

Time-wise, the Commandments can be placed in the Mosaic period and Moses is the most likely candidate for authorship. The biblical account of how they were written by God and rewritten by Moses is a highly imaginative way of asserting that God is their source and authority.

Their Uniqueness. Numerous law codes were in existence in the Near East at the time of Moses' promulgation of the decalogue. Twentieth-century digging has uncovered fragments of at least six incomplete collections:

1) Sumerian laws (Lipit-Ishtar)—2050 B.C.

2) Akkadian laws (Code of Eshnunna)—1925 B.C.

3) Babylonian laws (Code of Hammurabi)—1728-1686 B.C.

4) Hittite laws—17th century B.C.; written form, 13th century B.C.

5) Assyrian laws—15th century B.C.; written form, 12th century B.C.

6) Neo-Babylonian laws—7th century B.C.

With the exception of the last named, all of these collections are older than that of the Israelites.

The Ten Commandments are Israel's distinct contribution to legal lore. Unlike the *casuistic* law of the extra-biblical codes, Israel's Commandments are *apodictic*—that is, they are unconditional. Casuistic law begins with the introductory conditional element: "*If* so and so does this action, *then* the following penalty is in order." But the Commandments state without condition: "Thou shalt" or "Thou shalt not" do such and such.

A second distinction can be observed in Israel's rendering of the fourth through the 10th Commandments. These precepts, unlike the first three, deal with man's relations with other men. Precepts like these are found in earlier codes, but unlike other Near Eastern codes, violation of these precepts is considered a crime against God himself, not merely a crime against one's fellow man.

Their Place in Liturgy. The Commandments are generally found in a series because they were recited at the climax of the festival celebrating the renewal of the Yahweh-Israel covenant. It was within cult— that is, within worship—that Israel worked out the nature of her response of obedience to Yahweh. Israel's response to these Commandments was thankfulness and praise:

> The law of the LORD is perfect,
>   refreshing the soul;
> The decree of the LORD is trustworthy,
>   giving wisdom to the simple.
> The precepts of the LORD are right,
>   rejoicing the heart . . . .
> The ordinances of the LORD are true,
>   all of them just.

> (Ps 19:8ff; see also Ps 119)

A Brief Analysis. Israel did not consider the ten words as a *full* exposition of morality. In between idolatry, murder and adultery, there is a whole field of moral action demanding regulation.

We might say this of the ten words: they cover marginal situations extremely displeasing to Yahweh. The acceptance of Yahweh consists *at minimum* in abstaining from these offensive actions.

Two forms of the Commandments are given in the Bible: Exodus 20, from the Priestly tradition, and Deuteronomy 5:6-21. The first is in all likelihood a later reformulation of an older and simpler rendition. This Exodus 20 version will be discussed in the following paragraphs.

The enumeration of the Ten Commandments by various religious groups is not uniform. Modern Jews divide them in one way; modern Greek and Reformed Churches follow another division; Roman Catholics and Lutherans still another. The Roman Catholic/Lutheran enumeration is used in what follows:

The first commandment (Ex 20:2-6). Her neighbors might boast of many gods, but Israel's distinction lay in the recognition of one God alone. In further differentiation from her neighbors, Israel did not "carve idols . . . ; bow down before them or worship them. You saw no form at all on the day the LORD spoke to you," Moses says in a commentary in Deuteronomy 4:15,16. To this day modern archeologists have found no image of Yahweh in excavated sites.

Originally, the first commandment most likely read, "I the Lord am your God. You shall have no other gods besides me." Later additions reflect a borrowing from the Hittite suzerainty covenant. (Hittites: An Indo-European people who settled in Asia Minor before 2000 B.C. Their presence, power and influence extended into Mesopotamia, Syria, Egypt and Palestine.)

Such covenants/treaties usually open with a preamble—in which the Great King identifies himself. Then follows an historical prologue in which prior relationships between the covenanting parties—king and vassal—are reviewed. Next come the terms or stipulations which state the obligations imposed upon the vassal. Provision is made that a copy of the covenant/treaty be placed at the vassal's shrine and read regularly in public. Finally, various gods are called upon as witnesses and sanctions—blessings and curses—are supplied.

The Israelites were convinced that theirs was a covenant union with Yahweh. Therefore, they patterned this first covenant *word* after the manner of a familiar covenant form: 1) Yahweh identifies himself; 2) Yahweh recalls his benefits to Israel; 3) Yahweh sets down the first stipulation of the covenant: Israel shall have no other God but Yahweh. Further stipulations binding Israel are found in the remaining nine *words*.

The second commandment. Neighbors might chant divine names to support curses or magical formulas, but not so Israel. Likewise, the perjured use of the name of the Lord was forbidden. In later times, a deep reverence for the name of Yahweh led to the use of *Adonai*—"my Lord"—as its substitute.

The third commandment. The Sabbath was probably already observed when this precept was put in its present form (see Ex 16:23). No particular ritual is ordered; the commandment simply sets apart a period of time for the Lord. In order to keep the day holy, neither man nor beast is permitted to labor.

This is done in imitation of the Lord who "rested on the seventh day from all the work he had undertaken" (Gn 2:2).

The fourth through the 10th commandments. Commandments one, two and three involve man's relations with God. The rest focus on man's relationships with his fellowman.

First is the obligation to parents. This divine precept is universal in scope: every person, whether adult or child, must honor his or her parents. The fourth is the first commandment to promise a reward as motivation: "that you may have a long life."

Human life is sacred. The fifth commandment in forbidding murder aims to protect that sacredness. Neither war nor capital punishment was at issue in this law when formulated 23 centuries ago.

The sixth commandment—the prohibition of adultery—protects the sanctity of marriage. Of course the Hebrews considered the wife to be the property of her husband. Therefore only the rights of the husband could be violated.

The seventh commandment protects the sanctity of private property. Some scholars also see the commandment as forbidding the enslavement of free Israelites by force.

The eighth commandment forbids perjury—that is, false testimony—not only in legal actions but in any false statement against a neighbor. Here, *neighbor* means any person with whom an Israelite had contact.

The ninth and 10th commandments forbid unlawful desires. Such desires could well lead to actions already covered by the sixth and seventh commandments. When the ninth says, "You shall not covet your neighbor's house," *house* includes the goods within the dwelling as well. In desert dwelling days, *tent* might well have been the word used. (Note that both house *and* wife are considered as property!)

Prophets and the Law

Though the early prophets often took as their starting point the Law and Israel's failure to faithfully fulfill it, they were not concerned with law in itself. Their concern—amounting, at times, to a kind of agony—was Israel's response to the Lord in the here and now situation—*whether or not* that response was covered by the law. According to these early prophets, what pleased the Lord was not slavery to the commandments but the seeking of the *good:*

Seek good, and not evil,
    that you may live;
Then truly will the LORD, the God of hosts,
    be with you as you claim! (Am 5:14)

Israel's sin lay not in the breach of this or that commandment but in her complete failure before her God. For Amos this failure necessarily led to judgment:

You alone have I favored,
    more than all the families of the earth;
Therefore I will punish you
    for all your crimes. (Am 3:2)

God had chosen Israel. He had involved himself in her saving history (see Hos 11:1ff). But Israel was paying no heed to the Lord's saving action. She despised his gifts and refused to follow his way.

Isaiah saw Israel's failure manifested in her lack

of faith during the holy wars. The Lord—not large armies or better armaments—would conquer Israel's enemies, Isaiah insisted. But Israel continued to rely on her own defenses, refusing salvation on God's terms. Therefore he had no alternative but to purify his people.

By the time of Jeremiah and Ezekiel (seventh and sixth century B.C.), prophetic reflection on *torah* yielded a new insight: To a people given over to wickedness and stubbornness and infidelity to Yahweh, the Law has become judge and destroyer.

Israel was utterly incapable of fulfilling the Law. Either from lack of will or lack of power, she had become hardened in her opposition to the will of God.

Yet even here, the prophet saw cause for hope. This impasse will be solved by a new obedience which the Lord will place within his people's power. A new miracle would be wrought—not in the world of nature but in the heart of man (see Jer 31:31ff).

In Ezekiel, the Lord says: "I will give you a new heart and place a new spirit within you, taking from your bodies your stony hearts and giving you natural hearts. I will put my spirit within you and make you live by my statutes, careful to observe my decrees" (36:26,27).

Josiah's Reform

There were certain periods in Israel's history when the Law was given special prominence. During the latter part of the seventh century B.C., the ancient Oriental civilizations—after thousands of years—were coming to an end. A premonition of doom, a sense of insecurity prevailed throughout the Near Eastern world. A longing for the "good old days" prompted a great backward glance. The contemporary Pharaoh, for example, attempted to recapture the glory of the Pyramid Age. And Assyria's Ashurbanapal had myths and epics of ancient Babylon copied and collected into a great library.

Judah, in the south, did not escape this international experience of uneasiness. Though Assyrian power was weakening and Judah was enjoying a moment of freedom, a premonition of judgment hung heavy. Times were dangerous. Yahweh was surely needed at this moment. A guarantee of security was sought in a return to ancient traditions.

Two prophets, Zephaniah and Jeremiah, spearheaded the movement. They prepared the way for a reform credited to Josiah, Judah's young king (640-609 B.C.) In this spirit of returning to ancient roots, Josiah set himself to the task of repairing the Temple. During Temple repairs, a long-forgotten code of law was discovered (see 2 Kings 22). This "book of the law," most likely some form of the book of Deuteronomy, spoke with a mighty voice to Judah's present predicament.

Ultimately derived from the days of early Israel, *the book of the law* stemmed from the sanctuary at Shechem, the legal center of the north. When Israel fell to the Assyrians in 721 B.C., the Levite priests carried their legal traditions to Jerusalem in the south. There Temple priests eventually reedited them and brought them in line with southern traditions. Laid aside—"hidden"—during the days of less worthy kings, a reading of this reedited *book of the law* caused great alarm among the authorities who guided the young king.

The book brought into sharp relief the nature and demands of the Sinai covenant, somewhat over-shadowed in the south by the Davidic covenant and its theology (see treatment in Chapter 4). If God in fact demanded more than a mere reliance on his promise, Judah was playing a fool's game expecting him to leap automatically to her defense. Current efforts at national reform must grow into a full offensive, they insisted. The nation must return to an appreciation of Sinai and its "conditions." Yahweh's demands must be met.

In response, Josiah consistently purged foreign cults and their personnel; magic was suppressed; worship was centralized in the Temple.

Through this ancient law code newly-discovered, Yahweh again spoke a revelatory word: Drastic reforms were in order for his people. Through the book of the law, Sinai was revisited by a new genera-tion with its anxieties and fears, its hopes and faith in a God who loved in purest fidelity.

Unfortunately, this impetus to reform was short-lived. Fearing that the absence of Assyrian power would leave the field wide open for Egyptian domi-nance, Josiah went to do battle with Necho of Egypt at Megiddo. There, Josiah met his end. Jeremiah praised Josiah in these words:

He did what was right and just. . . .
Because he dispensed justice to the weak and
poor,
it went well with him. (Jer 22:15-16)

Under Josiah's son, Jehoiakim, the reform lapsed. Pagan practices crept back and public morality deteriorated. Though some nobles supported Jeremiah in his continuing efforts at reform, the cause was lost. Confident that the Temple, Jerusalem and Judah were secure in God's covenant with David, the demands of the covenant at Sinai were once again allowed to fade into the background.

Exile and the Torah

In Chapter 4 we rather hurriedly followed the nobles, priests and scholars of Judah into exile in Babylonia. Just as hurriedly, we followed the return of a remnant some 50 years later in 537 B.C. to rebuild a fragment of the former kingdom. But these 50 years in exile had an important role to play in Israel's future.

Without a land or political structure, the Babylonian exiles still had their *torah,* their priestly instruction, to live by. The priests of Israel had always been specialists in the law. In exile they promptly set themselves to the task of editing, purifying and simplifying existing liturgical and moral traditions.

The product of this priestly effort is known today as the Sacerdotal Code—that is, the code of the priests. It is characteristic of this Sacerdotal Code that its authors often place the origin or institution of a law in an historical event. Thus, the blessing of Noah and his sons is followed by the prohibition of eating flesh with its lifeblood (Gn 9:1-7). And the law of circumcision is attached to the making of a covenant by God with Abraham (Gn 17:9-14). Other laws of a cultic/ritual nature are assigned to no particular event but are attributed to Moses and included in the body of laws centered around Sinai.

Taken as a whole, the priestly work recalls the conditions, meaning and spirit of the covenant. It gathers up the memories of Israel, whose God was ever active on her behalf. Indeed, God had set up his tent in the midst of his people. The history of Israel's laws signified his presence.

Once again the covenant gave rhyme and reason to Israel's new situation—this time, the exile. With a law of their own, the exiles were still able to maintain a national and religious consciousness which set them apart from the people among whom they dwelt. Because of their law, Israelites did not eat the same as everyone else, they distinguished the sacred and the profane, kept special holy days, practiced circumcision, and were strict about the laws of marriage.

Concern for the law was very much a part of the exiles' continuing faith in Yahweh and his promises. It helped preserve their will to live as a distinctive people. Thus when return to the "promised land" became possible under Cyrus of Persia in 537 B.C., a "new exodus" was underway.

The reality to which the exiles returned was stark indeed in contrast to the build-up given them by the prophet we now call Second Isaiah. The homeland was poor and devastated. It teemed with economic and political problems. To the north dwelt hostile Samaritans; to the south the unfriendly people of Edom. Disillusionment, loss of fervor, poverty and warfare from the north delayed the rebuilding of the Temple for 20 years.

Nearly a century after the resettlement, Nehemiah, a Jew at the court of the new Persian king, learned of the deplorable condition in the province of Judah. Distressed, he approached the king and asked permission to go to Jerusalem and rebuild its walls for defense purposes. His plea was eventually heard, and he was appointed governor. By 440 B.C. he was in the city taking charge of affairs.

Nehemiah, though blunt and peppery of temper, was a just and able governor. In a *material* sense, he saved the community by bringing it political status, administrative reform and physical security. His efforts to *spiritually* restore the community were not so successful, however.

This spiritual restoration was tackled around 428 B.C. by Ezra, "the priest, scribe of the law of the God of heaven" (Ezr 7:12), an exile and a member of the Persian civil service. His charge, according to the "copy of the rescript which King Artaxerxes gave Ezra the priest-scribe" was ". . . to supervise Judah and Jerusalem in respect of the law of your God" (Ezr 7:14). The king's approval and signature on the rescript continued and extended the policy of his predecessor. The Persians were tolerant of native cults and insisted only that they be kept in order by responsible authority.

Ezra's goal was twofold: 1) a reorganization of the worship community; and 2) a strict reformation based on the law book, that is, on legal sections from the Pentateuch. (Just which laws these were scholars hesitate to say definitely.)

Appealing to the law (no doubt Dt 7:1-4), Ezra compelled the divorce of "the men of Judah and Benjamin" from their foreign wives. He climaxed his work at the Feast of the Booths in Jerusalem in the year 430 B.C. by reading "from the book of the law of God" to the people gathered together in Jerusalem (Neh 8:8).

With the reform of Ezra and the place it accorded to the Law, something new was emerging. Israel had always belonged to the Lord. Of her the Lord had said, "my people," and she had been proud of her identity among the nations. Increasingly, however, the Jew was to be recognized—not primarily because he was born a Jew or because the Lord acted in his history. No, he would be recognized by his adherence to the Law: "All . . . who have separated themselves from the peoples of the lands in favor of the law of God . . . join with their brethren who are their princes, and with the sanction of a curse take this oath to follow the law of God which was given through Moses . . . and to observe carefully all the commandments of the LORD" (Neh 10:29,30).

From Sinai on, the covenant bond between Yahweh and his people had been formative of the community. Now, with the approval of the Persian government, the Jews—no longer a political entity—took the oath to follow the law of its God (Neh 10:30). Thereby they obtained status as a recognized community permitted to handle its own internal affairs according to the law of its God. Henceforth, not covenant love but law constituted community.

From the period of Ezra on, therefore, law assumed an aura of authority. Growth from within gave way to adherence to law, an external thing. In a way, the history-making epoch—the period of God's "busyness" with Israel—had been terminated. Maintenance of the *status quo* through a meticulous expansion of the Law by its leaders, the scribes and Pharisees, became the norm of Jewish life. Within this new norm the history of Judaism has endured even to the present day.

Jesus Christ, whom Christians believe to be the destination of all Old Testament history and theology, took up his own history within this Judaism dominated by the Law. His role in salvation history was not do to away with one iota of the Law but rather to lead mankind beyond it—to enable men to break free of the Law and to broaden their personal horizons of goodness. This he did by bringing the Law to its fulfillment, that is, to its fullness of expression, in his own person.

Because the Jews, with few exceptions, could not integrate into their faith this new element brought by Jesus Christ, they rejected him. Judaism as a religion continued along its traditional path. Those who could accept this fuller understanding of the Law— not as restrictive but as guide to a greater freedom in the service of God and one's fellowman—followed a new way: Christianity.

Study Guide for Chapter 7

The Law, a Dynamic Movement in Israel

1) For Israel observance of the Commandments was a matter of life or death. *To live* meant to grow, to unfold, to be open to God, to place one's self-fulfillment at the service of others. In this light, discuss Deuteronomy 30:19,20. Could this way of choosing life be valid for today's Christian as well as for the Jew?

2) Sinai was a living experience, ever unfolding as responsibilities grew and obligations became more complex. Could we, by analogy, liken this to the broadening of the marriage experience? Qualify your answer.

3) In the Old Testament, "to be faithful" to God meant to be faithful to the law of the covenant. Read Exodus 20:1-12. How often is "Lord, your God" repeated? Suggest the significance of this repetition.

4) Read Exodus 20:1-12. Then read Genesis 3:4-6, no doubt written later. The acknowledgment of Yahweh as God stands as the basis of man's moral attitude. What would you say of the attitude of the woman and the man toward God?

5) Read Exodus 22:20 to 23:12. Note the level of these humanitarian laws. Read Exodus 23:12—a law requiring rest on the seventh day. What is the reason given here? What is the reason given in Exodus 20:8-11?

6) For the Greeks, *to sin* meant to go against a law of nature. For the Bible, *to sin* was to go against the God of the covenant. Look at Exodus 32:9; 33:3,5; 34:9. What word is dominant? Then read Deuteronomy 10:12-22—a homily calling for a change of heart, an unbending of the stiff neck.

7) Read Jeremiah 31:31-34. The covenant has been broken. In a new covenant the Lord will put his will into the hearts of men. What kind of new man does Jeremiah foresee? Will a call to obedience still be necessary? Explain.

8) Read Deuteronomy 6:5. This is *the* basic law. How is *love* deepened and widened? Read Leviticus 19:18b. Suggest why Jesus likened the two laws.

9) Later generations of Israelites examined current problems in light of God's self-revelation at Sinai and the covenant. What are some current problems confronting our nation today? What

are some current problems confronting youth today? Do you feel that the constant or basic elements of the Sinai covenant are valid today? Explain your answer.

10) Judaism has lasted for more than 24 centuries. What reason can you suggest for this phenomenon? Would you consider the "separateness" of the Jews as a value or disvalue? Qualify your answer.

So God said to Solomon: "Because you have asked for this—not for a long life for yourself, nor for riches ... but for understanding so that you may know what is right—I do as you requested. I give you a heart so wise ... that there has never been anyone like you. ...''

1 Kings 3:11-12

Chapter 8

Wisdom:
An Approach
to the Good Life

To that giant of a leader, Moses, Israel attributed its law. To a somewhat lesser giant, Solomon, Israel ascribed most of its wisdom. This crediting of literature to a person more famous and important than the real author was customary among the ancient sages. Through this device they drew attention to the writing and emphasized its value. Israel, by connecting its wisdom literature with Solomon, the prototype of the wise man and the Lord's anointed king, also affirmed its belief that these books were holy and divinely inspired.

Wisdom literature was preceded, naturally, by wisdom itself: a *practical* knowledge of the laws of everyday life and of the world. Wisdom was based on experience. Through observing human events, the wise man was able to discern a certain pattern (order, law) in human affairs. His insight was then molded into a pithy saying. For example,

A cheerful glance brings joy to the heart;

good news invigorates the bones. (Prv 15:30)

Such a saying or formulation gradually achieved the status of a maxim. Its purpose was to make living easier, to promote the good life. Each man need not risk all the pitfalls of life; distilled wisdom was at hand to steer him through most of its confusion.

The Origin of Wisdom. It was among Israel's neighbors—Egypt, Arabia, Edom, Mesopotamia—that wisdom literature had its origin. (Edom: a land which extended south of the Dead Sea to the Gulf of Aqaba.)

In each culture, wisdom was cultivated by a class of professional scribes who kept the records and administered the business of palaces and temples. The professional wise man would, no doubt, have emerged from the same milieu.

Instruction for life and conduct, guidance for dealing with men and affairs—this wisdom was passed on from teacher to pupil. At court, where royal officials were educated, many a schoolboy copied maxims while learning the equivalent of our A B C's. Thus they committed to memory such maxims as:

Hatred stirs up disputes,

but love covers all offenses. (Prv 10:12)

Wisdom literature entered Israel when David imported Egyptian scribes to assist in the administration of his kingdom in the 10th century B.C. Solomon became its patron. Aware of the international character of wisdom, Israel was, nonetheless, lavish in the praise of her own wisdom: "Solomon surpassed all the Cedemites and all the Egyptians in wisdom" (1 Kgs 5:10).

In addition to Israel's borrowing from the wisdom of her neighbors, a kind of homespun wisdom had also developed even before David's importation of Egyptian scribes. This earlier wisdom is called *gnomic (gnome:* a short, pithy expression of a general truth). Some examples: "From the wicked comes forth wickedness" (1 Sm 24:14); and, "Fathers have eaten green grapes, thus their children's teeth are set on edge" (Ez 18:2).

Wisdom literature enjoyed its golden age in Israel after the Babylonian exile when prophecy had declined. The maxims of Solomon and several other wise men were gathered to form the Book of Proverbs at the end of the fifth century B.C. The books of Sirach, Job, Ecclesiastes, Qoheleth and the Canticle of Canticles soon followed. About 100 years before the birth of Jesus, the Book of Wisdom marked the end of this golden age. The books of Tobit, Baruch and Daniel, as well as certain Psalms, all written well after the period of the exile, bear a likeness to wisdom literature. (See Pss 1,32,34,37,49,112,128.)

Uniqueness of Hebrew Wisdom. After the salvation history of Genesis and Exodus or the writings of the prophets, the reader senses a very different world when turning to the wisdom books. Gone are the denunciations of false worship and references to the covenant. Absent is the spirit of nationalism and messianic hope. Sparse is the talk about God, the Temple and worship. Wisdom literature, on the other hand, is filled with discourse about man, his character, his failings, his conduct, his weaknesses. Some may be tempted to ascribe wisdom to a purely secular mindset, divorced from the religious faith and worldview which shapes the rest of Old Testament writing. But Israel's characteristic faith in Yahweh distinguishes Hebrew wisdom from that of its neighbors, just as it distinguishes Israel in her sense of history and her practice of prophecy.

The neighbors could speak of the "good life," but Israel valued the "good life *under the law*." Characteristically, the neighbors' wisdom was ethical in a matter-of-fact way; after the exile, Israel became even more adamantly moral and ethical—its starting point was the knowledge of God and familiarity with his revelation and Commandments. The neighbors' wisdom remained in the realm of the secular; Israel's gradually assumed a deeply religious tone. Ultimately, Israel affirmed that there was no wisdom without *fear of the Lord*—the tending of the person toward God through love and obedience. A reading of the introduction to Proverbs alone is sufficient to well document this statement (see Prv 1—9).

Of all Old Testament literature, wisdom alone is explicitly attentive to the problems of the individual. In fact, it is the not-so-important man's business of living which is of particular concern to wisdom. Life is unity and wholeness; through wisdom it is preserved unshattered: "A wise man's knowledge wells up in a flood,...A fool's mind is like a broken jar—no knowledge at all can it hold" (Sir 21:13).

That wisdom could be acquired by attentiveness

to a master was recognized by Israel. Yet this was but an intermediate stage in wisdom's transmission. The original source or giver of all wisdom was Yahweh:

> For the LORD gives wisdom,...
> He has counsel in store for the upright....
>
> (Prv 2:6-7)

Wisdom in Israel traveled a long road, indeed. It had its origins in the court. But by the close of the second century B.C., wisdom was identified with the law of Moses (see Sirach 24:18-22):

> All this is true of the book of the Most
> High's covenant,
> the law which Moses commanded us....
>
> (Sir 24:22)

In the following section two of the wisdom books, Proverbs and Job, will be discussed briefly.

The Book of Proverbs

Proverbs is a book which should be read in small portions and slowly digested. Each meter or strophe holds the distilled wisdom of centuries of experience and observation. Read hastily its good things run together and become blurred.

Proverbs boasts 31 chapters. Though the introduction gives full credit to Solomon, its contributors are myriad, and much of the contents can be dated after the Babylonian exile.

A breakdown of the content shows the following structure:

1) a nine-chapter Introduction extolling the value of wisdom;
2) two sections definitely assigned to Solomon

(10:1—22:16 and 25:1—29:27): "The Proverbs of Solomon";

3) the words of Agur and Lemuel, apparently Arabians;
4) "Sayings of the Wise";
5) a section titled "Numerical Proverbs";
6) and a eulogy of the ideal wife.

Each section evidences a series of revisions by a traditional school of learned scribes. Here again, as in numerous Old Testament books, there is tangible witness to the living-growing-developing nature of Israel's literary works.

The book was finally compiled after the Babylonian captivity. Thus Proverbs came into being at a turning point in Israel's history. Apathy, individualism, immorality and exploitation of the poor were the order of the day. Organized worship and a highly codified law were in danger of reducing the faith to externals. The prophets, who for centuries had served as spokesmen for Yahweh, were silent. The post-exilic community of Judah was in a state of spiritual want. Into the breach stepped the wise man, the principle counselor and teacher in post-exilic Judaism. Now in him the charismatic spirit—always so vital a factor in Jewish fidelity to Yahweh—was present to the community (charismatic spirit: the spirit of the Lord). He heeded the signs of the times, assessed the needs of the people, and in response, taught the way to happiness (see Ps 119).

The wise man could take pride in the privilege his profession granted him: he could delight in the law of the Lord and meditate on it day and night (Ps 1:2; see also Ps 19:8-11).

Indeed, the wisdom teachers and the scribes—

those astute students of the law in post-exilic Judaism—were probably members of the same social class. Sirach 38:24, 33 and 39:1-11 give ample reason to postulate this relatedness. Ben Sira was a scribe with a school of disciples. Likewise Ezra "was a scribe, well-versed in the law of Moses" (Ez 7:6).

The Address. The words of the wise man are addressed to his son:

> Hear, my son, your father's instruction,
> and reject not your mother's teaching....
>
> (Prv 1:8)

The expression is figurative. The actual relationship is that of teacher and pupil.

Reward and Punishment. The wise men of Israel had great faith in the justice of God. In the early post-exilic period, however, there was still no concept of life after death. Thus, for these early wise men, there was no other place than the present life for Yahweh to manifest his justice. Blithely, one might even say rashly, the wise men promised riches, honor and a long life to those who would heed his instructions. These blessings were the companions of humility and national and personal fidelity to the law of God.[1]

Fear of God. Human wisdom without *fear of God* is futile. This is the principle which solidly situates the teaching of the entire book: "The fear of the LORD is the beginning of knowledge; wisdom and instruc-

---

1. Though Prv 15:11 admits that "The nether world and the abyss lie open before the Lord," it is only in the much later Wisdom 3 (early 1st century B.C.) that the wise man states that blessed immortality is the reward of the just.

tion fools despise" (Prv 1:7). No cowardly fear, this "fear of the LORD" is a devout awe which manifests itself in loving obedience to God. It sums up the meaning of religion, it describes the attitude of reverence before God.

Wisdom as a Woman. Already in the Introduction, wisdom is personified as a woman who goes about the street calling for disciples. Her message, like that of the prophet, is a *public* one addressed to the common people and the rulers at the city gates. She warns those who reject wisdom: "I, in my turn, will laugh at your doom; I will mock when terror overtakes you" (Prv 1:26). Wisdom's final note, however, is gentle: "He who obeys me dwells in security, in peace without fear of harm" (Prv 1:33).

Familiar Items. Several of the proverbs sound familiar notes to the modern ear. So commonplace is their usage, we tend to forget their venerable lineage.

For example, the adage, "Man proposes but God disposes," was an ancient one even in Solomon's time. Solomon's version goes like this:

In his mind a man plans his course,

but the LORD directs his steps. (Prv 16:9)
An even more ancient edition offered by Amen-em-ope, an Egyptian wise man, says: "One thing are the words which men say, another is that which the God does" (about 1100 B.C.).

The "Sayings of the Wise" incorporate the antithesis of a maxim old yet ever new: "Spare the rod and spoil the child." Proverbs puts it like this: "Withhold not chastisement from a boy; if you beat him with the rod, he will not die. Beat him with the rod, and you will save him from the nether world" (Prv 23:13,14). Sumerian wisdom, which dates back as far as 2400 B.C., contains this version: "If I strike you, my son, you will not die, but if I leave you to your own desires (you will not live)."

Proverbs of Solomon. Two collections of the maxims of Solomon constitute a hefty portion of Proverbs. In the first section (10:1—22:16), 375 short proverbs or aphorisms follow one upon the other in haphazard fashion. Each is distinct. All presuppose that justice and wisdom are synonymous; likewise, wickedness and folly:

> The lips of the just know how to please,
>> but the mouth of the wicked, how to pervert.
>>> (Prv 10:32)

The second collection (25:1—29:27) was edited and added to by the men of King Hezekiah's court in the eighth century B.C. (see Prv 25:1). This collection attests to the wise man's reliance upon the Law and the prophets:

> Without prophecy the people become
>> demoralized;
>> but happy is he who keeps the law.
>>> (Prv 29:18)

Irony characterizes several of these proverbs. One can sense a certain impish satisfaction in such sayings as,

> It is better to dwell in a corner of the
>> housetop
>> than in a roomy house with a quarrelsome
>>> woman.   (Prv 25:24)

The ethical is very much of concern to the wise

man Solomon and to the wise men who write and
edit in his name:

> The just man has a care for the rights of
>   the poor;
>   the wicked man has no such concern.

(Prv 29:7)

The Ideal Wife. Proverbs closes with 31 verses
devoted to a panegyric of the ideal wife. The verses
offer a noble model of womanhood for imitation by
the Jewish woman. As in much of wisdom literature,
the message appears to be purely secular. But the
whole piece receives a kind of religious consecration
by the second last verse: "the woman who fears the
LORD is to be praised" (Prv 31:30).

The Book of Job

Some scholars would put Job in a class by itself,
but because it is concerned with a profound
theological problem underlying the human situation, we have chosen to include the book under the
heading of wisdom literature.

The problem over which Job anguishes remains a
universal problem: *the enigma of the suffering of the
innocent.* Scarcely a day passes without our over-
hearing the repeated question, "Why?" The manner
in which one human being, the author of Job, grap-
pled with this, perhaps 2,400 years ago, is worth
consideration.

Job was an ancient legendary hero known to both
Babylonians and Egyptians. The Jewish author uses
Job as the model of the suffering just man. He is the
protagonist in a psychological drama. Before our

eyes Job unfolds his character in response to a crisis situation.

Only in Judaism, among the ancient world religions, did the problem faced by Job demand such finesse in the handling. In a world of many gods, capriciousness of the divinity was a ready solution. Evil and suffering could be laid at the feet of the gods just as easily as could good. But for the Israelites, there was but one God, the Creator, who is always turned toward men to do them good and bless them. He is, indeed, a God of justice. Reward and punishment are within his sphere of action; but the depth of his kindness must remain undisputed.

Over the centuries Israel reflected on this question, and a succession of answers to the problem of suffering were arrived at:

1) In early Israel the justice of God had traditionally been reduced to a mathematical formula. God rewards the good; God punishes the wicked. We could write the equations something like this:

good + good + good . . . = reward by God

evil + evil + evil . . . = punishment by God.

But, in fact, the wicked sometimes prospered; the innocent sometimes suffered.

2) Jeremiah, in the seventh century B.C. (and other later prophets as well), made bold to dispute the question with God:

Why does the way of the godless prosper,

why live all the treacherous in contentment?

(Jer 12:1)

Goodness did not always pay off. Why?

Isaiah 53 offered one understanding of why the innocent person suffered: "Yet it was our infirmities that he bore, our sufferings that he endured" (Is

53:4). Isaiah's innocent man was a suffering servant. Through his suffering he "shall justify many, and their guilt he shall bear" (Is 53:11). He suffered vicariously—that is, in the stead of sinners.

3) Another solution to the problem arose in the second century B.C.: reward and punishment meted out by God *beyond* the grave. The author of Job knew of a kind of afterlife (the nether world) in which good and bad shared a kind of shadowy existence. But an afterlife in which the scales of God's justice weighed out personal reward or punishment was a theological development after his time.

As for life and death, Job's contemporaries had their own interpretation. Many years, numerous children, an accumulation of material things, health and a reputable name constituted the reward of the good: This was life. Few years, no posterity, a disgraced name and a lack of necessities constituted the punishment of the wicked: This was death.

It was in this context that Job faced his dilemma.

The book of Job is easily divided into two sections: In a prose section (1, 2 and 42:7ff), the author appropriates an older folktale based on the legendary Job and uses it as a frame for his original poetic section (3—42:6). The book can be dated somewhere between 600 and 300 B.C., with the earlier date being the more probable.

The Prologue. Two scenes, one in heaven and one on earth, make up the prologue. In the first, Job's innocence is affirmed. He is a blameless and upright man. In the second scene, Job, despoiled of all earthly treasures—even of his health—is seated among the ashes. His friends are around him mourning as if he were already dead.

The Speeches. In a shocking speech Job breaks his silence and curses the day on which he was born (3:3). In rapid-fire order his friends defend the goodness and justice of God. Job has done evil, they are certain. There is no other explanation for his sufferings. Repentance is in order:

> If you set your heart aright
>> and stretch out your hands toward him,
> If you remove all iniquity from your conduct,
>> and let not injustice dwell in your tent,
> Surely then you may lift up your face in
>> innocence;
>> you may stand firm and unafraid.

(Jb 11:13-15)

Desperately, Job protests his innocence, spells out the extent of his righteousness. In a final plea, with human wisdom bankrupt in the face of evil, he boldly challenges the Almighty to answer him. And address him God does—out of the storm.

The Lord's Answer. The Lord does not defend himself. He merely counters human wisdom with the grandeur of the divine wisdom which fills, supports and maintains the universe. Here is mystery, indeed. Despite paradox after paradox, the world does not fall into chaos.

Yahweh teaches well. Only in such a divine/human encounter can the problem of evil be broached. Only here is the man of faith granted an insight into the reality of God. Then, he accepts good, accepts evil—both from the hand of the Lord. In humility, he prays with Job:

> I have dealt with great things that I do not
>> understand;
>> things too wonderful for me which I cannot
>> know.
> I had heard of you by word of mouth,
>> but now my eye has seen you.
> Therefore, I disown what I have said,
>> and repent in dust and ashes.   (Jb 42:3-6)

The "solution" offered by Job is not an altogether satisfying one. It removes the problem from the category of the mathematical and places it within the realm of mystery.

Man is too little to question the providence of God. Divine wisdom must be reverenced though its workings are obscure to human reason. Man must trust God's goodness and justice. He has no right to plumb fully the secrets of the divine will. Humility and awe and adoration best describe man's stance before God. After all, it is the glory, the power of God's providence which sustains the whole of creation.

The Epilogue. The prose epilogue bears a divine scolding for the accusers of Job. Before the Lord Job's claims are true: he is guiltless. The book, however, does not abandon the traditional principle of retribution. This could not be. After all, it is founded on the conviction that God looks to the moral order of things and is the just ruler of his world. Hence, Job's prosperity has to be restored, even enhanced.

The story, however, has modified the accepted principle in one regard. The Lord can test the virtue of the just man by sending suffering. Then, finding the sufferer faithful—even purified—amidst trials, he will reward him generously.

Despite Yahweh's speech and Job's humble conclusion, Judah must wait for a deeper and fuller insight into her problem: the paradox of the suffering of the innocent.

The Book of Wisdom: A Bridge Between Old and New

So far as the Old Testament is concerned, the last piece of wisdom literature to be produced was the Book of Wisdom. Composed in Egypt around 100 B.C., the author's purpose was to encourage his fellow Jews who were suffering persecution at the hands of apostate—fallen away—Jews.

The book is largely concerned with rewards and punishments after death and its author witnesses his thorough familiarity with earlier Old Testament writings. But of particular interest to us is the fact that wisdom teaching had advanced to the point where it would serve as a bridge between the Old and the New Testaments.

For example, St. Paul, whose letters are considered the earliest biblical writings of the Christian era, surely reached back into Wisdom in his effort to describe Jesus in Colossians 1:15: "He is the image of the Invisible God, the first-born of all creatures" (see Wis 7:26). And another verse from Wisdom—

For from the greatness and the beauty of
created things
their original author, by analogy, is seen.
(Wis 13:5)
must lie at the base of Paul's statement: "Since the

creation of the world, invisible realities, God's eternal power and divinity, have become visible through the things he has made" (Rom 1:20).

John, too, reached back into Wisdom for vocabulary and illustrations that would help him express concepts and doctrines sacred to the Church founded by Jesus. For example, Wisdom's "You who have made all things by your word" (9:1) found fuller and quite majestic expression in John's introduction to his Gospel:

> In the beginning was the Word;
>
> . . . and the Word was God . . . .
>
> Through him all things came into being . . . .
>
> The Word became flesh . . .
>
> and we have seen his glory:
>
> The glory of an only Son coming from the
>> Father. (Jn 1:1,3,14)

And in expressing the conviction that man's search for immortality had ended in Jesus, John makes no drastic break with Old Testament faith. Rather he undergirds the greater and more profound revelation of the New Testament with a statement from Wisdom:

> For to know you well is complete justice
>> and to know your might is the root of immortality. (Wis 15:3)

John's profession of faith runs,

> Eternal life is this:
>
> to know you, the only true God,
>
> and him whom you have sent, Jesus Christ.
>
>> (Jn 17:3)

In Jesus Wisdom had truly reached its full flowering and most perfect expression.

Wisdom and Beyond

1) 1 and 2 Chronicles are two of Israel's history books. Read 2 Chronicles 1:7-12, the dramatic story which tells of Solomon's prayer for wisdom (also in 1 Kgs 3:5-14). What other gifts are included in wisdom?

2) The early Church used the Book of Sirach extensively in presenting moral teaching to catechumens and the faithful. Read Sirach 3. What moral teaching stands out in this chapter? In the light of your own moral training, how much of the wisdom of Sirach 3 is valid for today?

3) Certain psalms bear a likeness to wisdom literature. Read Psalm 34:12-23. How does God deal with the man who has learned the "fear of the LORD"? Would most of your contemporaries derive comfort from the wisdom teaching of verses 18, 19 and 20? Give a reason for your answer.

4) For Israel there was no wisdom without "fear of the LORD." What does "fear of the LORD" mean for you? Read Proverbs 3:1-12. How does it describe "the demands" of "fear of the LORD"? Does God expect too much of man? Give a reason for your answer.

5) Wisdom offered happiness/salvation here and now. Read Proverbs 2. Draw up a list of the things which the wise man included in the notion of salvation. Would the contemporary Christian also consider these as constituting salvation? Why or why not?

6) Read Proverbs 14. Find at least six maxims which show the author's concern for morality. What immorality was he protesting in each instance? What would you say of the level of morality called for? Is the morality based on fidelity to commandments or on worthy human relationships? Which would you consider a more truly human approach? Why?

7) Read Job 1. Note the sufferings heaped on Job. Read Job 31, which reflects the theology of Job's day: God rewards the good; he punishes the wicked. Job knows that he is innocent. He examines his conscience and yet finds no fault in his behavior. Do you feel an empathy with Job? Why? In what way is Job's insight satisfying or dissatisfying to you?

8) Read 2 Corinthians 5:6-10. Compare Paul's theology about reward and punishment with that

of Job. Do the same with Romans 2:1-11. Also, Matthew 16:27. Read Peter 2:21-25. What does Peter say about the suffering of the innocent Jesus?

The days are coming, says the LORD, when ... I will raise up
for David a just shoot; he shall do what is right and just in the
land.

Jeremiah 33:14-15

Conclusion

Chapter 1 surveyed the complex situation within and out of which the early Israelites embarked upon their personal saga with Yahweh, their God. Chapters 2—8 followed the dynamic progress of the faith of this people of God as they moved (through history) from the initial Sinai covenant event to the point at which Judaism emerged.

The purpose of this conclusion is to rapidly sum up the political/geographic and religious situation of the Jews as the Lord leads them—and the world—toward the dawn of "the last days," that is, to the Messianic era (Acts 2:17).

Political/Geographic. In the course of his military exploits, Alexander the Great brought Persian supremacy in the Near East to an end. Then followed a period of more than 150 years during which the Jews in their remnant of a promised land were dominated by the Greeks.

In 166 B.C. Judas Maccabeus—member of a family of priestly lineage—led his energetic and zealous people in a successful revolt. The ensuing period of comparative independence lasted until the coming of Pompey to Jerusalem in 63 B.C.

In the interim John Hyrcanus I (134—104)—high priest, general and ethnarch of the Jewish commonwealth—extended the frontiers until they were practically the same as they had been in the time of David. Of note to Christians is the fact that his son, Aristobulus, gained power over Northern Galilee which he Judaized. (*Judaized:* forced to follow the practice of the Jewish religion.)

Internal struggle brought about the intervention of Rome in the affairs of the land. Pompey, who was forced to besiege the Temple (63 B.C.), accepted Hyrcanus II as high priest—and therefore, as ruler—and Palestine became part of the Roman province of Syria.

Religious. For all their national and religious solidarity at this time, the Jews were not a united people. In their attitude toward the Law and the Temple, notable differences appeared. At least three "sects" were visible: the Pharisees, Sadducees and Essenes.

The Pharisees kept strictly to the Jewish customs of diet, circumcision, fasting and prayer. Yet they were willing to adapt the Law to the changing conditions of life and to accept doctrines not found therein, such as the resurrection of the body and the apocalyptic—the future—Kingdom.

The Sadducees accepted the Law or Torah but rejected the body of oral law gathered around it. They denied the resurrection and argued against belief in angels and demons and predictions about the time to come—end-time.

The Essenes considered themselves as the true Israel which would survive the tribulations of end-time. They formed a community separated from the world to devote itself to the Torah and to await the hour when God would establish the apocalyptic Kingdom. The Essenes were also devoted to the notion of the holy war which would purify the land of pagan culture and set up a Holy Land.

Even the above brief analysis of the sects demonstrates that there were new and diverse thoughts running through the Judaism of the last two centuries before Christ. One thing, however, was certain: Belief in one God, that is, monotheism, had triumphed. Judaism had room for but one Supreme Power or Lawgiver who ruled over all creation.

Nonetheless, the popular hope that her God would give Israel victory over all her enemies and establish her under his rule in endless happiness underwent a radical change. Though increased stress on the Law contributed to a kind of static condition—that is, to a lessening of the sense of history—Israel's hope must continue forever. Hope was central to Israel's faith.

A concept, therefore, that comes to the fore at this final stage in the consideration of Israel's religious situation is "eschatology"—the doctrine of last things. Under this heading we can describe

Israel's radically altered form of hope: Judaism expected a catastrophic intrusion of God into its present and the emergence of a new age. Sirach 36:1-18 cries out for that moment: "Hasten the day, bring on the time. . . . Fill Zion with your majesty . . . . Reward those who have hoped in you. . . . Thus it will be known . . . that you are the eternal God."

As the Old Testament period drew to a close, the eschatology of Judaism was expressed in a literary form called apocalyptic. (*Apocalypse:* revelation.) Daniel in the Old Testament and Revelations in the New Testament are the two major biblical examples of this kind of writing, but the form was a popular one.

Though the expectation of a political Messiah was not abandoned, the Messiah tended to merge in the apocalyptic literature with the coming of the heavenly deliverer in the end-time.

This messianic king would not conquer the world by the sword. As "son of man" he would receive from the Ancient One—God—"dominion, glory and Kingship" (Dn 7:14). Before his advent all hostile powers would be overthrown, judgment would be "pronounced in favor of the holy ones of the Most High" (Dn 7:22) and

> Then the kingship and dominion and majesty
> of all the kingdoms under the heavens
> shall be given to the holy people of the Most
> High. (Dn 7:27)

In its affirmation of the everlasting Kingdom— that is, of a new world beyond history—Israel confessed its faith that no matter how hopeless the present scene, God is ruler. His reign is supreme.

Meanwhile, sustained by hope in a joyful future, the Jews diligently applied themselves to the observance of the Law. They must not be found wanting in the Final Judgment.

With these considerations our look at the Old Testament is brought to a conclusion. An important aim of *God Calls a People: A Journey Through the Old Testament* will be achieved if it can make it easier for Christians to approach the question, "Who is Jesus of Nazareth?" For it is only in continuity with the hopes and strivings of the Jewish people and their faith that we can dare to answer with the earliest Christians: "God has made both Lord and Messiah this Jesus" who was crucified and raised up again (Acts 2:36).

169

Illustrations

p. vi   *Moses With Tablets of the Law,* woodcut, 1955, by Jakob Steinhardt. The Cincinnati Art Museum, Gift of Dr. Leon Kolb to the Mr. and Mrs. Ross W. Sloniker Collection of 20th Century Biblical and Religious Prints.

p. 4   *Astarte,* Judaean terracotta, 9th-6th c. B.C. The Cincinnati Art Museum, Gift of Dr. and Mrs. Nelson Glueck.

p. 24   *Moses Receiving the Tablets of the Law (Exodus 20:21-22),* color lithograph, 1956, by Marc Chagall. The Cincinnati Art Museum, Mr. and Mrs. Ross W. Sloniker Collection of 20th Century Biblical and Religious Prints.

p. 36   *Abraham's Sacrifice,* woodcut, 1962, by Cyril Satorsky. The Cincinnati Art Museum, Mr. and Mrs. Ross W. Sloniker Collection of 20th Century Biblical and Religious Prints.

p. 60   *Joshua,* lithograph, by William Gropper. The Cincinnati Art Museum, Mr. and Mrs. Ross W. Sloniker Collection of 20th Century Biblical and Religious Prints.

p. 78   *Noah Offers a Sacrifice to God After the Deluge (Genesis 8: 20-21),* etching, by Marc Chagall. The Cincinnati Art Museum, Mr. and Mrs. Ross W. Sloniker Collection of 20th Century Biblical and Religious Prints.

p. 96   *Moses and Aaron,* etching, by Marc Chagall. The Cincinnati Art Museum, Mr. and Mrs. Ross W. Sloniker Collection of 20th Century Biblical and Religious Prints.

p. 118   *Levi (Deuteronomy 33:9-10),* color lithograph by Charles Sorlier after Marc Chagall's design, 1962. The Cincinnati Art Museum, Gift of William Murstein.

p. 142   *King Solomon (I Kings 3:11-12),* color lithograph, 1956, by Marc Chagall. The Cincinnati Art Museum, Gift of Albert P. Strietmann to the Mr. and Mrs. Ross W. Sloniker Collection of 20th Century Biblical and Religious Prints.

p. 162   *King David,* color lithograph, 1956, by Marc Chagall. The Cincinnati Art Museum, Mr. and Mrs. Ross W. Sloniker Collection of 20th Century Biblical and Religious Prints.